THE TEN LORDS OF THE HENGE

Also by Alain Loriquer

Escaping the Lake of Darkness
The Third Branch of the Tree of Life
The White Plate of God

THE TEN LORDS OF THE HENGE

Alain J. Loriquer

The Ten Lords of the Henge

Copyright © 2013 Alain Loriquer

Cover art by Jean Carlo Jursich
Cover and interior design by RMcB Creative Services
ISBN 978-1483987217
Printed in U.S.A.

Table of Contents

The Ten Lords of the Henge

Introduction

Pleased with the Caraka's answer, the Ancient One nodded wisely as he added, "Yes, those amazing beings are learning just as you are. Even though they are perfect, they're accountable for the life-forms their love creates.

"Our experiences are part of their ever-growing worlds and are instantly absorbed into the energy we share with them. And just like any nurturing mother on planet Earth, they watch with great anticipation as their off-spring slowly learn how to fill themselves with love in order to return to their eternal home."

Feeling as if he was still missing a number of integral pieces of this extraordinary puzzle, the Caraka absent-mindedly said to himself, "The Ten Lords of the Henge are perfect, but the little beings they've created are not.

"Nevertheless, they accept responsibility for whatever happens. And with both perfect and imperfect beings, the worlds of God march on—to wherever they are going."

It was still all way beyond him. The Caraka smiled incredulously at his beloved Master. After all was said and done, everything around him appeared to be working fine. And that was all that really mattered to the humans of planet Earth and the Lords of the Henge.

Please join the Caraka as he continues his inner-world journeys high into the worlds of God—learning about the responsibilities of grand Creators and how they expect little Souls like us to do our part as their co-creators.

Dedication

This book is dedicated to the ten beings known as the Lords of the Henge. Their precious love, emitted in the form of sound, assures that all their off-spring join with them in the dance of eternal life.

THE MASTER OF
THE MIDDLE UNIVERSE

1

Beginning Again

Pleased to be finally starting eleven classes with a new mentor, the Caraka sat down in his favorite chair. For more than twenty-five years his Master, the Ancient One, had been guiding him throughout the inner worlds. As he journeyed to these amazing sites he was continually learning about the heavens of our Almighty Creator that await us all.

After agreeing to begin classes months ago, he had taken some time off. His previous inner-world journeys had greatly altered his level of consciousness and he was no longer the same. Feeling rested, he was now ready to continue.

The Caraka closed his eyes. Then he began filling himself with the feeling of love. Once this precious energy permeated his inner core, or Soul, he placed his attention on the light brown obelisk he had been guided to six months earlier.

The instant it came into focus, he thought of his beloved Master. This great being had taught him how to travel in the inner worlds and he would never forgot the unbelievable spiritual gift he had been given. With even greater appreciation for his upcoming classes the Caraka began studying the terrain of his new mentor's planet.

---

* In ancient India the Sanskrit word Caraka has had a number of different meanings. In the following stories the Caraka is the equivalent of a spiritual wanderer, seeker and student.

From his previous journey, he remembered that the beings of this world were one hundred and twenty feet in height. Their civilization was considered one of the most advanced of the physical plane and he felt honored to be studying here. Needing to locate his new Master, he continued scanning this desolate light brown world.

It reminded him of a rocky desert—a desert similar to the many found on his blue planet. Wondering if Earthlings could survive in this inhospitable environment, the Caraka placed his attention completely on the light brown obelisk a short distance away.

Acutely aware that he should have returned months ago, he slowly headed toward it. When he was less than twenty yards away, he stopped and called out, "Hello Master of the Middle Universe. Are you ready to receive a student from the Milky Way Galaxy? I'm really late. I hope you don't mind."

To his great surprise the obelisk began to shimmer like a giant sparkler. Then, it exploded hundreds of yards in every direction. Five Earth seconds later, a soft telepathic voice replied, "Welcome young one. As you just mentioned you are late, but this is of little importance.

"I am the Master of the Middle Universe. The Ancient One requested that I contribute to your spiritual education. Please approach the obelisk to use the elevator. It's located at the foot of the structure and will take you directly to our temple's inner sanctum."

Sensing everything was going well, the Caraka headed toward the giant obelisk. When he reached the elevator's triangular door, it melted away, allowing him to step inside. Because this elevator was quite different from any he had seen on Earth, the Caraka began to examine it.

Its cabin had nine equal walls. Somehow it had been carved out of what he assumed to be an enormous clear diamond. One of the nine sides served as the door. He stared through its clear form as the elevator descended into the bowels of the planet.

Surprised at how fast it could move, the Caraka noted that the elevator was not fixed on rails or tracks. Instead, it seemed to fly effortlessly through what appeared to be a white etheric energy.

With technology so much more advanced than anything found on Earth, the Caraka wondered what awaited him inside the temple's inner sanctum. Two Earth seconds later the elevator came to a stop. As before, the material of the clear door slowly melted away, allowing him to step into a brilliantly lit room.

The room appeared to be a giant cavern—a cavern filled with brilliant yellow light produced by a large number of yellow obelisks. Lining the room's outer walls, the obelisks' intense energy made it impossible for him to see.

Staggering a few feet forward, the Caraka realized it was foolish of him to go any further. Wondering how he should proceed, he listened closely as the soft voice of his new mentor called out, "Young student from the Milky Way Galaxy, welcome to the largest temple of the Middle Universe. I am its current Master and if you don't mind, I would like to pick you up in my hand to facilitate our conversation."

Surprised by the offer, the Caraka quickly assented, "I think that's a good idea. However, the light is so bright in here that I can't see where you are."

Remembering that it would take a while for the tiny Earthling to adjust to the sanctum's powerful energy, the Master knelt down. Then he replied, "I'm ten feet in front of you. My yellow skin matches the light of the room, so it's almost impossible for you to make out my one-hundred-and-twenty-foot body."

Feeling at a great disadvantage, the Caraka tried to remain calm as his new mentor's soft hand slowly encircled him. He watched with great curiosity as the Master gently raised him into the air.

Once he was eye level with this great being, the Caraka was able to gaze into the depths of the Master's massive, pale orange eyes. Finding them incredible, he timidly smiled and then watched as his new mentor began traversing the giant cavern.

Half an Earth minute later, the Master began to explain their surroundings. "This is the main room of our temple," he said. "I am normally close by, so I suggest we meet here to begin our classes. For your first visit I'm going to give you a short tour.

"Near the middle of the cavern is an open auditorium where millions of initiates of the Light and Sound routinely meet to share their love with one another. These spiritual travelers come from the Inner and Middle as well as Outer universes. They play a big role as the love of our Almighty Creator is slowly augmented on the physical plane. During your upcoming classes you will have a chance to meet a number of them.

"At the far end of the room, you will find entrances to the various cities of our ancient civilization. There are more than one hundred billions inhabitants on our planet. And all of us live underground.

"We were able to harness the energy of God million of years ago and lack for nothing. Food is grown on the enormous farms located on our surface, as well as on our satellite planets. It is regularly shipped to the various centers that prepare it.

"Since we are not worried about surviving, we spend most of our time assisting other areas of the physical plane. You wouldn't believe how many seekers there are on the physical plane—all eager to learn about the love of the Light and Sound."

Suddenly halting his discourse, the Master stared across the open auditorium in bewilderment. Then he said, "I'm sorry, but our brief tour must come to an end. A number of initiates are waiting for me on the other side of the room and I must go.

"Before I join them, I would like to assure you that it matters very little that you took some time off. I'm delighted you are here and looking forward to our classes."

Terminating their brief tour, the Master knelt down and carefully placed the Caraka on the ground. Then he smiled one last time, before taking off for the far end of the cavern.

Aware that the powerful energy of this amazing being had affected him somehow, the Caraka placed his attention on his home on planet Earth. Then he transported himself into the peace and quiet of his room.

The instant he arrived, he opened his eyes and calmly gazed out the far window. It was hard to believe, but his upcoming classes were going to be with a giant, hundred-and-twenty-foot Master who could hold him in his hand. Sensing they were going to be amazing, the Caraka smiled to himself in anticipation.

Inner sanctums dedicated to the growth of spiritual beings are located throughout the physical plane.

2

Agricultural Saints

Ready to continue his inner-world journeys with a hundred and twenty foot giant, the Caraka closed his eyes. Then he placed his attention on the temple of the Master of the Middle Universe. Seconds later, he found himself in the main room of the enormous site.

Adjusting his eyes more quickly this time, he saw that he was only a few feet away from the elevator he had taken on his previous visit. Pleased to be starting from a point he knew, he slowly scanned the brilliant room. To his amazement, the other side of the room appeared to be over ten Earth miles away, while its brilliantly lit ceiling glowed at least three miles above him.

Delighted to be seeing better this time, the Caraka called out, "Hello Master. I've returned for my second class. Are you close by?"

An instant later, the soft telepathic voice of his new mentor replied, "Yes, I'm in the center auditorium holding a small class. Please join us."

Delighted with the invitation, the Caraka continued into the brilliant light until he spotted the Master with twenty of his initiates. These students varied in size and shape. Five of them had humanoid bodies and were almost as tall as his hundred and twenty foot Master. Three were large reptiles close to twelve feet in height. The largest group consisted of tan-colored ants.

He counted at least twelve ants. And when they stood on their hind legs, the Caraka estimated them to be more than twenty feet in height. Easily the shortest of the group, the Caraka ducked in-between their enormous bodies to find a place at the Master's feet.

Pleased that his student from Earth had joined them, the Master continued, "We beings of the Light and Sound seldom recognize the sacrifices made by our predecessors—especially if their assignments are in a zone of extreme darkness.

"Life on the physical plane is never easy. Most galaxies are battle grounds and will continue to be battle grounds until the major cycle of the lower worlds ends. When this monumental event takes place, all of us will be called back to our Creator's Ocean of Love and Joy. Until then, we must all do our best to help each other grow spiritually.

"Not long ago, an old friend came to visit me. Appearing un-expectedly in his Soul body while I was conversing with a few friends in a nearby park, I instantly recognized that he was des-perate. He requested that I travel to his world immediately and I consented. Then he disappeared in the ethers of the site.

"Since he resides in one of the darker zones of the Outer Uni-verse, it had been ages since I last visited his world. He is currently in charge of twelve galaxies and the moment I was able to free myself, I sat down at the base of a tree where I frequently meditate. Then I closed my eyes and projected myself to his temple.

"The instant I reappeared, he ran over and reached up for me to pick him up. With my curiosity piqued, I knelt down to gently lift his tiny body to my face. When he was at eye level I was over-come by the excruciating pain he was in.

"With tears of despair flowing down his cheeks, he blurted out, 'I'm so happy you are here. We were recently attacked by war-riors of the dark light and very few of us remain. They took mil-lions of us as slaves and vowed to return for more.

'Only our temple remains because it is hidden deep in the mountains where few of them dare to go. We are all frightened and have no idea what to do.'"

Stopping to look into the faces of his students, the Master could see they were all listening intently. He continued, "The natives of my friend's planet are yellow in complexion and stand close to twelve feet in height.

"Famous for two things, they are known as excellent farmers, unrivaled for sharing their love with everyone they meet. They are considered harmless. With three suns nurturing their enormous planet, they harvest multiple crops on a continual basis.

"Finding it strange that the beings of the dark light had taken a large percentage of their population away, I decided to find out why. I placed my friend on the ground. Then I told him I needed to take a short walk.

"When I was certain I was alone, I sat down and placed my attention on the uprooted farmers to find out where they were. The instant I spotted them, I realized that a spiritual miracle had taken place.

"The beings of the dark light need farmers. They had transported them to a planet at the center of their civilization. Currently ruling thirty percent of the Outer Universe, these relentless warriors plan to conquer the rest of the Outer Universe in short order.

"Without being aware, the rulers of these dark warriors have placed these carriers of the Light and Sound in a position to share their love with them. It will be difficult for the farmers at first. But once their new rulers get accustomed to having them around, they will be allowed to live as they always have.

"As all of you know, workers that supply food are very important in every society. For this reason, they will inevitably share their love with their capturers. Before we end this class, I would like all of you to consider how our Creator moves its little children to where they are needed.

"Beings that help others, especially in zones of darkness, always succeed. This is why the farmers were destined to live there."

His story finished, the Master looked down at the tiny visitor from planet Earth. Then he knelt down to pick him up. Looking directly into the Caraka's eyes, the Master added, "We have a few of those farmers on our planet's surface. Would you like to visit them? They were placed here a short while after our civilization moved underground. We've always appreciated what they do for us."

Delighted with the offer, the Caraka replied, "Sure, but how do we get there?"

Conscious that the Caraka tended to ask a lot of questions, the Master replied, "Patience little one, patience."

Then he took a couple of giant steps toward a massive support column a short distance away. Once there, the doors of a giant elevator melted away and the Master entered the enormous crystal cabin.

Earth seconds later the door closed behind them and the elevator began to move. When it reached the planet's surface, the Master stepped outside and the Caraka began to examine this amazing world.

As far as the eye could see stretched fields of a green plant that resembled corn. Close to fifteen feet in height, this plant grew unimpeded in every direction. Two hundred yards away stood a large building, and the Master began taking giant steps toward it.

Less than ten Earth yards from the building, his mentor announced, "Inside this massive structure are a number of the farmers I spoke about. They live here while caring for their precious crops.

"It just so happens that they are the ancestors of the farmers recently captured by the warriors of the dark light. They too grow food while sharing their precious love with anyone they meet."

Peering down from the Master's large hand, the Caraka spied a few farmers coming in from the fields. Although his knowledge of agriculture was limited, he knew it was difficult to dedicate one's life to feeding others. Wondering what motivated these ancient farmers to live in this manner, the Caraka studied them closely.

Hearing the Caraka's curious thoughts inwardly, the Master quickly added, "The hearts of these farmers are so filled with love that it is impossible for them not to share it with others. They are far more ancient than they appear. And their recently captured relatives, are fortunate to carry their precious genes."

Pleased that the Master had brought him here to the planet's surface, the Caraka continued scanning the precious crop growing far into the distance. Then his thoughts returned to the ancient beings who had planted them.

There were millions of farmers on his blue home, and he was certain that a large percentage of them loved their work. But he doubted that many of them would do it for free, as these being were doing.

Happy to have been invited to a section of the planet's surface that wasn't a desert, the Caraka turned to gaze into the Master's enormous orange eyes and said, "Thank you guiding me to these immense fields. These ancient farmers are truly a gift from God and I respect how they are able to give for the good of the whole."

Pleased that the Caraka was learning about the different types of beings living on the physical plane, the giant Master replied, "You and I, along with everyone else in the physical universe, know how precious they really are.

"This is why they were the perfect candidates to begin a colony of the Light and Sound in the middle of that dark civilization. With the vast amount of love they wield it is impossible for them to fail. Now little one, our class is over. Please return to your small blue planet."

Delighted to be studying with this massive being, the Caraka smiled one last time. Then he projected himself to his home. The moment he arrived, he opened his eyes and couldn't help but think about those loving farmers freely giving of themselves to everyone.

If, somehow, they were ever assigned to planet Earth in the future, he was certain that it would only be a matter of time before they were considered agricultural saints—agricultural saints planting their seeds and giving away their precious crops to keep everyone alive. Never expecting anything in return.

Beings of the Light and Sound who give their love to others in zones of darkness are precious beyond belief.

3
Going Off the Beaten Path

Exhausted physically, the Caraka sprawled out on his bed. It was late—almost ten o'clock. He wanted to sleep, but before he could call it a day, he knew he had to return to the temple of the Master of the Middle Universe.

Closing his eyes, he placed his attention on the temple's inner sanctum and transported himself there. The instant he arrived, his intuition told him that something unusual was about to take place.

Having learned to expect just about anything during these inner-world journeys, the Caraka curiously scanned the temple's enormous room, which appeared to be eerily abandoned.

Wondering what was going on, the Caraka calmly called out, "Hello Master. I've returned for another class. Are you here?"

All remained quiet and the Caraka decided to look elsewhere. Sensing his teacher might be in the center of the room—the Caraka headed that way. When he had traveled the equivalent of four Earth miles, he stopped.

In the distance, he spotted a large group gathering in the Master's indoor amphitheatre. Thousands of attendees were slowly walking down the circular site's gently sloped yellow floor and he wondered if the Master was among them. Hopeful, the Caraka continued in that direction.

The instant he arrived, he approached a being who looked to be an usher. This giant was almost as tall as his mentor. In order to get her attention, the Caraka strategically placed himself between her massive feet.

He cried out, "Hello up there. Can you tell me where I can find the Master of the Middle Universe?"

Surprised to see a tiny being from the Milky Way Galaxy addressing her, the usher joyfully knelt down. "Why, yes," she replied. "He's on the other side of the amphitheatre. Would you like me to take you there?"

Delighted by her offer, the Caraka gazed into her kind eyes and replied, "I sure would. If it isn't too much of an inconvenience."

Pleased to help the Earthling, the usher scooped up his tiny body into her hands and slowly lifted him into the air until he was level with her chin. Able to see much better, the Caraka watched curiously as she calmly maneuvered her immense body in-between the other attendees.

When they reached the other side of the amphitheatre she called out to a large being with his back to them, "Hello Master. This tiny visitor showed up at the entrance and was looking for you, so I brought him here."

Pleased that the Caraka had arrived, the Master immediately spun around. Then he reached out to accept the tiny Earthling's body. Now safely on the Master's palm, the Caraka watched joyfully as his mentor lifted him up to his face.

He listened closely as the Master whispered, "I felt your presence a short while ago, but it was impossible for me to go looking for you. There are more than three hundred thousand initiates of the Light and Sound attending our conference, and I'm scheduled to give a talk in a few minutes. If you don't mind I would like you to join me onstage."

Wondering if he had heard correctly, the Caraka unconsciously blinked a number of times while the Master stared into his eyes. Then he watched incredulously as the Master took three long steps toward the amphitheatre's center stage.

As he realized that this inner-world journey was forcing him to do something he really didn't want to do, the Caraka nervously called out, "This is a very unusual class. I don't know if I've been properly trained to go on stage with you. But if you think I can help you with your talk, I'll do my best."

Finding it humorous that his tiny student was losing his courage, the Master seemed to smile as he weaved among the initiates. Ten Earth seconds later, they stepped onto the stage.

The first thing the Caraka noticed was a ray of brilliant white light glowing brightly in the center of the stage. The Master made a beeline for it. Once its loving energy surrounded their bodies, the Master carefully raised the Caraka above his head with both hands.

Cognizant that thousands upon thousands of Initiates of the Light and Sound were staring at him, the Caraka wondered why he hadn't just skipped this class and gone directly to bed.

He listened closely as the Master's loud telepathic voice called out for all to hear, "Welcome everyone. As you can see, I have a special visitor in my hands. He is an Earthling who lives on a small blue planet located in the Outer Universe. He's currently taking classes at our temple, and I thank him for joining me on stage.

"Even though he feels uncomfortable at the moment, he accepted my invitation to help me with my talk. I think he is quite courageous, and for this reason he will be the centerpiece of my talk.

"You see, this tiny initiate of the Light and Sound comes from a small solar system in the Milky Way galaxy. His presence at our gathering gives you a good idea of what is happening in those far off worlds. He is a true seeker of God and like all true seekers he is not afraid to go off the beaten path."

Feeling the Caraka fidget in his hands, the Master slowly lowered him to his heart. Then he continued, "You initiates of the Light and Sound did not come to this gathering to stare at this tiny Earthling, but to help each other grow as spiritual beings.

"I would like to point out that all of us have the capacity to travel in the inner worlds of God just as he does. But how many of us actually do it? This little Earthling's presence should inspire all of us to place more attention on our spiritual journeys to help others. We, too, must have the courage to go off the beaten path.

"Please consider traveling to a world, such as Earth, in order to help the beings there understand that they are not alone. Take the time to visit the Anami Lok to sing with the higher world Angels of our Almighty Creator. Make an effort to visit the Ocean of Love and Joy to fill yourself with as much of God's benevolent energy as you can."

Planning this to be no more than a short welcoming speech, the Master lifted the Caraka up to his face. As he gazed lovingly into his tiny student's eyes, he called out for all to hear, "Thank you for assisting me, little one. All of us appreciate your efforts and hope more Earthlings follow you here."

Sensing this was the perfect time to leave, the Caraka nervously nodded his head in agreement. Then, he timidly whispered so that only the Master could hear, "Thank you for inviting me onstage, but I think it's time for me to go home."

With a quick shift of consciousness, the Caraka instantly projected himself to his bed on planet Earth. Seconds later, he opened his eyes, content to be alone in his room.

This inner-world experience was one of the rare times a Master had used him as an example—and it certainly had made him feel uncomfortable. But if it had helped a few of those advanced physical plane beings somehow, he was more than happy to be lifted in the air and stared at by thousands of spiritual giants.

Spiritual giants he doubted he would ever see again.

As Earthlings travel in the inner-worlds, they receive golden opportunities to come in contact with other beings of the Light and Sound.

4

The Pale Brown Light

Suddenly feeling as if he should explore the giant planet he was currently studying on, the Caraka placed its image in his third eye and calmly projected himself to the Middle Universe. The instant he arrived he spotted the light brown obelisk he had been guided to on a previous visit.

Sensing it was the best place to start, he headed directly toward the immense structure. Stopping a few hundred Earth yards away, he began to examine the colorful world surrounding him.

The planet's desert-like terrain was pale yellow in color and its flat surface stretched far into the distance. High above him were two of the planet's suns. One glowed a pale yellow, while the other emitted a soft purple light. The energies of both suns blended together effortlessly—forming a multitude of different colors.

Suddenly drawn to the obelisk, he looked in its direction and was pleased to see the Master of the Middle Universe emerging from the giant elevator he had taken during a previous class.

Delighted his student had arrived, the Master walked over and said, "I thought you might like to spend some time on the surface of my world. It's a beautiful planet and has served my people well.

"Eighty million years ago our ancestors needed the surface to grow food. We were growing rapidly and our ancestors made the difficult decision to live underground. From what I learned as a child, this was not an easy thing to do.

"Most of my ancestors refused to leave the surface. They cherished being able to walk on this yellow dirt, gazing at the stars above their heads. Never completely accepting the decision to leave, they reluctantly agreed to live underground. Hundreds of years later, they had adjusted, but were never really happy.

"Fortunately, the second generation after them had less of a problem. They easily adapted to the comfortable environment our engineers had created, permitting our society, based on the Light and Sound of God, to grow beyond all expectations.

"Semi-annually we hold a ceremony at the base of the obelisk to commemorate what our ancestors achieved. We give homage to the beautiful planet we call home and thank our leaders for having made the decision to live inside our planet. Below the surface there are vast theatres with enormous screens, which allow our entire population to participate. But it's never the same as being here in person."

Finding the history of his current mentor's planet interesting, the Caraka gazed into the eyes of his giant teacher as he asked, "Are there other planets in your solar system? Or is this the only one?"

Delighted to discover that the tiny Earthling was slowly remembering, the Master replied, "Our solar system is not large. There are a total of five planets, each populated by one hundred and twenty foot giants like me.

"Years after we were established underground, our ancestors placed a limit on our population. Four trillion was chosen as the ideal amount, and once this limit was reached it was clear that they had made the right decision."

Raising his right hand high into the air, the Master pointed out a large red object in the sky. Then he continued, "That planet is also part of our civilization. Five hundred billion of my brothers and sisters of the Light and Sound live there."

Intrigued by this red planet, the Caraka stared at it intently. He couldn't help but wonder if he had ever lived in this solar system in a past life.

Picking up his young student's inquisitive thoughts, the Master whispered, "Yes, little one, you've lived here before. Your home was on that red planet, and you were here when our ancestors made the decision to live underground. Would you like to visit the place where you lived?"

Delighted, the Caraka nodded his head up and down in anticipation. Then he watched as a pale yellow beam of light slowly engulfed their bodies. When it was strong enough to pick them up, he felt himself being propelled toward the red planet.

Thirty Earth seconds later, they were descending into a long valley nestled in among three large mountains. Contrary to the Master's sprawling plain-like world, this planet was quite mountainous. Its soil, red in color, was quite thin, and he doubted that very much could be grown there.

Off in the distance, the Caraka spied an immense orange river at least five Earth miles wide. He was surprised to see a light brown obelisk on its closest bank. Wanting the Caraka to learn more about this beautiful planet, the Master steered him toward the obelisk.

The instant they arrived, he pointed at the immense structure and said, "You lived less than a quarter of an Earth mile from here in a six sided home that has long been removed. You spent most of your youth playing with your friends on the banks of the river or meditating at the base of the obelisk.

"Obelisks are important symbols in our society. They reflect the power that the energy of our Almighty Creator wields and are located throughout the worlds of God.

"The pale-brown light emitted by this obelisk is a pacifier of energies. It has the capacity to neutralize the anxieties we carry around with us as we face the many challenges of the physical plane.

"Most beings of the Middle and Outer Universes live in areas of darkness. For this reason, they are constantly being tested. These tests come in the form of anger, lust, vanity, greed and attachment—with attachment being one of the hardest to conquer.

"Lifetime after lifetime, we return to this plane until we are able to master these difficult passions. When my ancestors were asked to live underground, they had a great encounter with attachment.

"All of them wanted to remain on the planet's surface. But it had gotten to the point where there were too many of us. Consequently, they were asked to detach themselves from what they loved. This was the only way our civilization could grow into the world we have today.

"In order to soften the separation, this pale-brown light was used to weaken my ancestor's desire to remain above ground. This soothing light is considered an antidote for attachment. In order for you to understand its magical properties, I suggest you experiment with it when you return to your home.

"Reflect on the most challenging problem you have at the moment and invite the pale brown light to help you resolve the situation. In no time at all, you will see a big shift in how you perceive your problem."

Delighted with the homework, the Caraka smiled at his new mentor with great appreciation for guiding him to the place where he had lived so many lifetimes ago. Then he realized he didn't quite understand what the Master wanted him to do when he got home.

Wanting a better explanation, he asked, "Why does the brown light dissolve attachment more than the other negative attitudes?"

Not at all surprised by the Caraka's question, the Master's eyes lit up as he replied, "The pale brown light vibrates at a special rate directly related to the negative virtue of attachment.

"As a child, every inhabitant of our world is taught that every passion can be vanquished by a special light. If I'm not mistaken, this subject has been addressed by a number of worthy teachers of your own planet.

"I suggest you familiarize yourself with these teachings in order to soften the complicated tests your world offers you. The information is there, but you must find it.

Now, class is over little one. See you next time."

Reluctant to leave, the Caraka gazed at the pale brown obelisk one last time. Then he slowly shifted his attention to his favorite chair on planet Earth. The instant he opened his eyes, he stared at the bookshelf on the other side of the room.

He clearly remembered purchasing a book that addressed the subject of color and light years ago. It had to be there somewhere. Hoping he hadn't lent it to someone or given it away, he walked over to the bookshelf and started looking.

Unbeknownst to Earthlings, the precious pale brown light of our Almighty Creator has the capacity to dissolve the negative virtue of attachment.

5

The Role of Obelisks
in the Worlds of God

After slowly awakening from a deep sleep, the Caraka suddenly remembered he had a number of commitments to fulfill. It was the beginning of a busy weekend and he knew he had to get up.

Wanting to get started on the right foot, he decided to do his morning exercise first. He carefully propped his pillow against the head board of his bed. Then he slowly sat up. Once comfortable, he closed his eyes and began to focus on the energy of the Master of the Middle Universe.

An instant later, he found himself in the temple's inner sanctum. A few yards from the elevator he had used on his first class, he stopped to adjust his vision to the bright light of the room.

Earth minutes later, he was able to see much better and began heading toward the center of the room. Halfway there, he spotted fifteen of the Master's initiates in the distance. Aware that they had spotted him before he saw them, he slowly approached them.

They were all staring at him. He wondered if it was because of his brief appearance on stage during his previous visit. Less than ten Earth yards away, the Caraka watched nervously as the two initiates closest to him slowly moved over, gesturing for him to join them.

Surprised by the invitation, the Caraka timidly called out, "Thank you for inviting me into your group. However, I need to find the Master. Have any of you seen him?"

The giant initiate closest to him immediately knelt down and gazed deeply into his eyes. "I know where he is," she said. "Would you like me to take you there?"

Appreciating the offer, the Caraka answered, "If you don't mind, I would really appreciate it."

With a big smile on her tranquil face, she gently scooped him up with her right hand and began to carry him across the room. When they had walked the equivalent of twenty Earth minutes, she exited the temple's inner sanctum and entered a corridor constructed of aquamarine colored stone.

On and on she marched until they came upon what resembled an enormous park. In this park were the tallest trees the Caraka had ever seen on the physical plane. Purple in color, their branches were filled with unusual looking birds. On the ground beneath them were countless animals—all in apparent peace and harmony with one another.

Some of these creatures appeared to be larger than the ancient dinosaurs of Earth's past, and the Caraka wondered if they were related somehow. Wanting to find out more about this magical site, the Caraka looked up at his gracious guide to ask her a few questions. But before he could, she motioned with her free hand for him to look ahead.

The instant he did, he spied the Master of the Middle Universe contemplating at the base of a giant tree. Seeing that his mentor's eyes were closed and his legs crossed, the Caraka watched intently as his companion quickly closed the gap between them. Happy to have carried the little Earthling to this sacred site, she deposited him at the Master's feet. Then, she gingerly backed away to rejoin her group.

Wondering how long he would have to wait to start his class, the Caraka stared into his mentor's serene face. The Master looked so peaceful that the Caraka didn't dare disturb him. Wanting to do the same thing, he sat down at the Master's side and closed his eyes as well.

Earth seconds later, he found himself in a bright blue world surrounded by towering mountains. Judging by the colors of the site, the Caraka concluded that he was at the border of the mental and etheric planes in the middle of a small valley. He looked up what appeared to be a dirt road and spotted the Master watching him.

Wondering why the Master had guided him there, the Caraka walked over and said, "I saw you sitting in the lotus position in the park on your planet and decided to focus on my third eye. I had no idea you would guide me here."

Appreciating the Caraka's desire to join him in the inner worlds, the Master replied, "Ever since I can remember the elders of my civilization have been training our children to travel in their Soul bodies. This has assured that all the members of my planet are able to visit the planes of God whenever they get the urge.

"I was on my way to visit a special site when I felt your energy calling out to me. Would you like to join me? It's only a short distance away."

Welcoming the invitation, the Caraka took a few steps forward and joyfully mounted onto the Master's outstretched hand. Then he watched curiously as his mentor began hiking up the dirt road that snaked between two multi-colored mountains.

After walking the equivalent of five Earth miles, the Master stopped in front of what could only be described as an enormous mound—a mound constructed of a clear diamond-type material. At its base was a twelve-sided entrance, and before the Caraka could ask where they were, the Master proceeded through it.

Inside, the Master raised the Caraka up to his face and said, "Earthlings like you travel to temples exclusively designed to give you the experiences you need, while we one-hundred-and-twenty-foot giants, travel to temples specifically designed for *us*.

"This temple was constructed eons ago, and I first came here when I was a small child. When it comes to the spiritual growth of its little creations, our Almighty Creator has thought of everything. Amazing schools have been established on every plane for every being ever created."

Spying a bright blue obelisk in the distance, the Caraka pointed in its direction while asking, "I see obelisks everywhere. They seem to be important for your people. Why is this?"

The giant Master grinned broadly as he replied, "The obelisk is a symbol for the power of the Light and Sound of God. It represents the energy that our Grand Creator provides to guarantee that all of its little creatures are alive and well.

"Wherever you find an obelisk, no matter what color it happens to be, you can be sure that a large influx of God's love is present. For this reason, temples of the Light and Sound are normally built a short distance from them.

"Obelisks also represent the energy that God utilizes to help us return to our eternal home. If you ever feel lost, look for the nearest obelisk. Then merge with its energy to return to the higher worlds.

Delighted to be learning about these majestic structures, the Caraka gratefully stared into his giant mentor's tranquil eyes. Then, he focused completely on the pale blue obelisk a short distance away.

As he observed its magnificent light, images of millions of smaller obelisks and temples suddenly appeared in his inner eye. Caught completely off guard by this unexpected vision, he came to a stunning realization.

Obelisks, and the temples that accompanied them, are the equivalent of rest stops placed at strategic sites on major highways. Like most rest stops, they're always open and available to serve the spiritual travelers that need to use their facilities.

Delighted to have made this discovery, the Caraka realized that his inner-world class had come to an end. He stared lovingly into the tranquil eyes of his giant mentor one last time. Then he calmly projected himself off the Master's hand to the peace and tranquility of his quiet home on planet Earth.

Thoughts of the busy day that lay ahead instantly assaulted him. But he rearranged his pillow and quickly overruled them. Seconds later, he began to replace those thoughts with the intense desire to locate the nearest obelisk.

Obelisks and the Temples of God accompanying them line the highways guiding spiritual travelers to their eternal home.

6

Meeting the Shark Master

Slowly climbing the steps to his room two at a time, the Caraka realized he was exhausted. It had been a hectic day. Wanting to complete his next inner-world journey before sitting down for his evening meal, he closed the door behind him and collapsed into his favorite chair.

Wondering if he even had enough energy, he closed his eyes to locate the Master of the Middle Universe. An instant later, he found himself standing in front of the elevator in the temple's inner sanctum.

Hoping this class would be a short one, the Caraka slowly scanned the room to see if there was anyone there. But it was empty. Remembering that his mentor had told him he was normally close by, he proceeded across the room.

When he reached the indoor amphitheatre where the Master held his classes, the Caraka peered down at the center stage. His teacher was sitting on the edge of the circular stage in contemplation.

Because this was the second time he had found the Master sitting in the lotus position, the Caraka assumed that his new teacher did this often. Not wanting to disturb him, he silently tiptoed onto the stage and sat down alongside him. Then he closed his eyes to merge with the Master's energy.

An instant later, he found himself being transported to another world—a world almost completely void of light. As he slowly acclimated himself to its darkness, he spied the Master's brilliant form less than fifty yards away. Eager to continue his class, the Caraka closed the gap between them.

When he was only a few inches from the Master's immense feet, he joyfully jumped up onto the Master outstretched palm. Securely clutched in the Master's hand, the Caraka watched with great joy as his teacher carried him toward a large, dark orange mound.

Stopping in front of the mound's entrance, the Master whispered, "Young Caraka, I am about to guide you inside an important temple of the lower physical plane. This site of the Light and Sound is fairly new and vital to the few advanced beings living on this planet."

The Master carried the Caraka through the building's round entrance. Coming to a halt in the center of the temple's enormous main room, he placed the Caraka on the floor.

Knowing his student was about to learn something of great importance, the Master said with great love, "I am going to leave you here. The Master of this temple is on his way to meet with you. He should arrive shortly."

Finding it strange that a temple of the Light and Sound had hardly any light, the Caraka stared into the Master's smiling face and watched him slowly fade into the ethers of the lower physical plane.

As soon as he was alone, the Caraka began to scan the dismal world surrounding him. It was so dark that it was almost impossible for him to see anything clearly. Wanting to ameliorate the situation, he began altering his inner vision.

When he finally reached the right frequency, he was surprised to see an orange ball glowing in the center of the room. It reminded him of a large pumpkin, and seemed to be the only source of light in the room, barely illuminating the temple's dark green walls off in the distance.

The Caraka could see that the building was crudely constructed—so crudely constructed that fear began to overtake him. Strongly sensing that this class in a lower physical plane temple might be dangerous, the Caraka hoped he wouldn't have to stay there very long.

Ten Earth seconds later, he spied a dark green figure heading his way. This being appeared to be about the same height that he was and when it was less than five feet away he saw that it resembled a shark with short legs.

Aware that the Caraka was watching its every move, the Master stopped and said, "Welcome young traveler. Welcome to our temple. As you have already observed there is very little light here. For this reason you must be very careful whenever you visit our site.

"I am a being of the Light and Sound, but I make every effort to hide my energy. To accomplish this, I routinely cover myself with this protective coat."

After slowly scanning the room to make certain they were alone, the Master cautiously opened his outer garment to reveal his brilliant white light. Then he closed it instantly.

Having shown the Caraka his true energy, the shark continued, "Our planet is located on the outskirts of the physical universe and is only a few million years old. Almost all of the inhabitants living here are young Souls with much to learn."

"Not long ago, I attained Mastership on the mental plane. After passing this milestone, the Masters of the Light and Sound assigned me here. I'm scheduled to return to this planet for three consecutive incarnations, and I must say that living here has been quite a challenge.

"My goal is to help the few spiritual seekers of the planet recognize the importance of the love of God and what it can do for them.

"Recently, our small group carved out this enormous temple

in the largest mound we could find. Up till now, we have been left alone, but things change quickly in this dark green environment."

"Our world could be compared to the oceans of your planet. Existing in an extremely dark scenario, where the big fish eventually eats the little fish, everyone must be constantly on guard.

"Fortunately, there are plenty of large sea worms crawling around at the moment—so the majority of the inhabitants living here are well fed. However, if these worms fail to reproduce at their current rate, my friends and I could end up being meals for one of the larger bands of enormous shark-like beings that roam the area."

Aware that the oceans of Earth were similar, the Caraka asked, "How can you help someone appreciate the love of God when you know you might be their next meal? Your assignment in not an easy one."

The Master of the Dark Green Temple seemed to crack a small smile as he replied, "You're right. It's not easy. But I do my best. Fortunately, I made an important discovery upon arrival.

"Whenever a female shark delivered an offspring, I noticed that her heart would open for a short while. Wanting to take advantage of this aperture, I sought out birthing mothers and tried to be with them for this event.

"Hours after the magic of a birth took place, I would delicately point out the love they had for their newborns. Most of the female sharks were able to recognize this love, and I urged them to share it with others. A few of them found it easy to do.

"In order to help them grow as spiritual beings, I insisted that we stay together as a group to share our love with each other. Before too long, a few of the males showed up. Greatly enjoying the energy we were emitting they quickly joined our group as well.

"Now there are close to five thousand of us sharing our love with one another. We are steadily growing, which is why we decided to build this temple."

Amazed by what this small shark, shrouded in protective garb was doing, the Caraka came to the realization that its assignment was not only difficult, but almost impossible. Finding his current tests on planet Earth quite easy in comparison, he stared compassionately at its serene green face.

Understanding that he had discovered why the Master of the Middle Universe had guided him to this dark site, the Caraka smiled at the shark Master with gratitude for all that it was doing to teach others about the love residing deep inside them.

Then he said, "I must return to my home in the Milky Way Galaxy. But before I go, I want to tell you that I greatly respect what you are doing. Don't give up! You and your shark initiates of the Light and Sound are doing a great job."

Grateful for the words of encouragement, the Master nodded his head in appreciation. Then he watched as the Caraka placed his attention on his room on planet Earth and disappeared in the ethers of the temple.

Once he opened his eyes, the Caraka realized how fortunate he really was. Sure, his day at work had not been the easiest. But he didn't have to worry about being eaten all the time.

Suddenly grateful for the blue planet he lives on, the Caraka smiled in appreciation for everything he had. And unlike the rookie Shark Master of the Lower Physical Plane, he didn't have to hide his love or light in protective garb in order to survive!

Unbeknownst to humans, the birthing of life is a recognized aperture—vital for the spreading of love in the darker worlds of the physical plane.

7

Invasion of the Twenty-Foot Penguins

Completely awake, the Caraka sat up in his bed. It was three a.m. and for some reason he found it impossible to sleep. Needing to calm down, he took twenty deep breaths. Noting a distinct difference, he made his way to his favorite chair in hopes of quieting himself even more.

After making himself comfortable, he closed his eyes and began chanting his favorite mantra. Moments later, he projected himself into the inner sanctum of the Master of the Middle Universe's Temple.

Instantly appearing in front of the site's elevator, he began scanning the enormous room. To his amazement it was filled with a countless number of spiritual pilgrims. Wondering if he was seeing correctly, he blinked twice before continuing to scan the room.

As he looked closer, he could see that these inner-world travelers had very distinct bodies. The largest ones were so big that even the Master of the temple had to look up to them, while the smallest were half the size of a human from planet Earth.

Some were humanoid, while others resembled mammals and reptiles. A large percentage were strange looking creatures he had never seen before. Wondering why they were assembled in the temple, the Caraka decided to search for his new mentor.

With great caution, he meandered through the crowd. As he did, he could feel the immense love these beings were sharing with one another. Their inner hearts were wide open and he could tell they were doing an excellent job connecting with the essence of their Almighty Creator.

As the Caraka continued his unbelievable inner-world journey, he spied the Master of the Middle Universe at the perimeter of his indoor amphitheatre. Surrounded by a group of giant penguin type beings that looked to be close to twenty feet in height, the Caraka was delighted he had found him so easily.

Less than ten Earth yards from the Master, the Caraka could tell he was in a serious conversation with the penguins. Seeing that his student from Earth had arrived, the Master quickly nodded in his direction. Then he returned his attention to the penguins surrounding him.

Wondering what was happening, the Caraka listened closely as the Master replied, "I'm sorry that your Master was attacked by a large band of dragons. He was a good friend of mine and I will sorely miss him.

"As all of you know, he was an amazing teacher and always did a great job making sure his students were well connected to the Light and Sound of our Almighty Creator. This is why I'm certain one of you is more than qualified to replace him.

"What concerns me is that these tenacious dragons have reappeared in your galaxy. They miss very little and know you are unprotected. I've recently learned that they've overrun two other colonies of the Light and Sound in the adjacent solar system. Now they control that sector completely.

"Since they know there are large pockets of penguins still remaining on your planet, we must assume they will return. Before they do, I suggest you find a good place to hide until things calm down.

"Your outpost is located in an area of the Outer Universe where change is inevitable. For this reason, I also suggest that you connect yourselves with the essence of our Almighty Creator as often as you can.

"This will help you survive until the dragons learn that their actions have consequences. Good actions bring about good results, while bad actions bring about karmic consequences that must be repaid. Sooner or later, they will figure this out."

Certain the penguins understood his simple message, the Master smiled upon them with great compassion. Then he sensed he had left something out and continued, "Living in the Outer Universe is never easy. But eventually the dragons will grow spiritually and everyone will benefit.

"Eight hundred thousand years ago, a flotilla of their ships attacked two of our planets. In response, we did nothing but watch. Hoping they wouldn't be foolish enough to attack again, we waited to see what would happen next.

"Days later, they returned to raid a nearby civilization. The inhabitants of that civilization happened to be one of our strongest allies. And the moment I heard about the attack, I knew the dragons had made a strategic error.

"At the time, our neighbors were not spiritually inclined. They considered themselves physical plane warriors and took these aggressive strikes personally. With no remorse whatsoever, they wiped out all the dragons in their solar system.

"Since we one-hundred-and-twenty-foot giants have been pacifists for eons, we did nothing but watch. We no longer considered ourselves physical plane warriors and incurred very little karma.

"From what I know of the penguins of your galaxy, you aren't warriors either. You are advanced beings of the Light and Sound and I recommend the following. The moment you return to your temple, invite all the initiates of your planet to participate in a number of large-scale exercises.

"Have them meet at their sacred sites, and request that they ask for protection from their Almighty Creator. If they all reach deep inside themselves in unison, they will get results."

While considering the Master's advice, the twenty-foot penguins began swaying back and forth in unison. Then their temporary leader stepped forward and said, "Thank you Master. We will do as you say. As you know, it is difficult to organize penguins on a large scale, but we will do our best."

Determined to continue living on their planet, the penguins nodded their heads in gratitude for what the Master had shared with them. Then they slowly waddled away while the Caraka looked upon them with great compassion.

Once they had disappeared in the crowd, the Master peered down at his tiny student from Earth and added, "If this had taken place on your planet, you humans would have handled the situation in a different manner.

"Like the dragons, you consider yourselves warriors and would have done your best to defend what you consider is yours. For this reason, your civilization would have been annihilated.

"The penguins however, will survive. They have no desire to be drawn into an unnecessary conflict. Once the dragons conquer them, they will consider the penguins weak and not feel threatened.

"Eventually, the dragons will come to the conclusion that it is in their best interest to ignore them. Even the most savage beings of darkness know better than to destroy adversaries that do little to defend themselves.

"Now, this gathering will last for the equivalent of one Earth week. I suggest you return as often as you can. There are amazing beings assembled in our inner sanctum and once you get to know a few of them you will better understand how our universe is slowly expanding."

Pleased that the Caraka was now aware of the inter-galactic event taking place in the temple, the Master smiled directly into his tiny eyes. Then he marched off to another meeting.

As his enormous mentor disappeared in the crowd, the Cara-ka recognized that it was time for him to go home. It was at least three thirty a.m. on Earth, and he hadn't forgotten that he had to get up for work in a few hours.

Placing his attention on his favorite chair, he instantly projected himself there. The moment he arrived, his thoughts turned to the twenty-foot penguins recently attacked by the dragon warriors.

Hopefully they would survive their invasion without suffering excessively—thereby permitting their non-violent civilization of the Light and Sound to continue growing in peace.

Passive civilizations incur very little karma—while aggressive ones are eventually destroyed.

8

Receiving a Pagoda Statue

The next day, the Caraka sat down on his bed. He found it impossible to forget that there were millions of spiritual seekers gathered at the Master's temple. He wanted to return there as quickly as possible.

He propped up his pillow behind his back, and the moment he was comfortable, he placed his attention on his third eye and projected himself to the inner sanctum.

An instant later, he stood in front of the diamond elevator where he normally started his classes. To his great joy, the interplane visitors were still there. Appreciating the opportunity to observe them, he slowly made his way toward the Master's amphitheatre.

A third of the way there, he passed alongside a large herd of woolly mammoths joyfully conversing among themselves. Then a group of giant, white grasshoppers crossed his path. Stopping to admire them, he noticed the effervescent energy they were emitting.

Once they left him behind, he ran into a number of nebulous-looking life forms he never seen before. Wondering where they resided on the physical plane, he stared at them in amazement.

Eventually he reached the area where the Master and his initiates always gathered. Not to his surprise, a large number of the one-hundred-and-twenty-foot giants were mingling there with their guests.

Eager to locate his teacher, he timidly looked up at the giant initiate closest to him. "Hello!" he called out. "Can you please tell me where I can find the Master of the Middle Universe? He requested that I participate in this event and I need to find out what he wants me to do next."

Caught off guard by the tiny Earthling standing between her feet, the giant immediately kneeled down and said, "I recognize you from the opening ceremony when the Master held you in his hand during his talk. I have no idea where he is right now, but I can help you find him if you want."

Grateful for the offer, the Caraka joyfully replied, "Thank you. With your height, we should be able to spot him easily."

Hoping the student from Earth was right, the giant initiate reached out and carefully scooped him into her right hand. Then she headed toward an enormous alcove of the temple he had never visited before. As she glided between the attendees with amazing grace, the Caraka shook his head in disbelief at how fast she was walking.

When they reached the far end of the alcove, the Caraka could see they were heading toward what appeared to be a violet, crystal pagoda. This immense pagoda however, was much different from the pagodas found on Earth. It was shaped more in the form of a pyramid and appeared to have thousands of floors.

Estimating that the three bottom floors could easily accommodate two hundred thousand of the inhabitants of this planet at a time, the Caraka wondered how many beings of the Light and Sound were currently inside.

Hearing the Caraka's loud, inquisitive thoughts, his giant escort said, "Once our ancestors made the decision to live underground they constructed this building. Because they had very sophisticated technology at the time, they were able to complete it on schedule.

"On the day of its inauguration, all the inhabitants of the planet were invited to attend the grand opening. From the legends passed down to us, this giant structure was finished at exactly the right time.

"Within hours, invaders from the other side of the Middle Universe attacked us. Anticipating this attack months before, the elders of our civilization had asked for volunteers to remain on the surface to act as decoys.

"They made up almost a third of our population, and unfortunately these brave beings were annihilated by our enemies' brutal weaponry. Convinced they had won a strategic battle, the enemy took off for another planet, completely unaware that two thirds of our population was hidden underground.

"This pagoda stands as a tribute to the bravery of the volunteers who lost their lives and the new world we were forced to accept close to three million years ago. Now, we have become so accustomed to living underground that none of us would ever consider returning to the surface."

Having finished her brief narrative, the Caraka's escort glided through the pagoda's main entrance. Once inside, he immediately spied the Master of the Middle Universe surrounded by a small group of visitors.

He appeared to be finishing up a talk, and when the Caraka was less than thirty yards away, he heard the Master say, "We beings of the Light and Sound greatly appreciate the spiritual commitment of others. For this reason, we would like to give each of you a small present in appreciation for everything you have done while on the physical plane."

Reaching down into a large bag, big enough to accommodate two compact cars, the Master pulled out a small crystal replica of the violet pagoda. It was nearly four feet in height, and with great love, he presented it to a thirty-foot beetle to his right.

Then he pulled out another and presented it to one of three woolly mammoths to his left. On and on the Master reached into the bag until each member of the group had received a statue.

When he was finished, the Master joyfully smiled as he said, "Thank you for all you've done over the years. The Masters of the spiritual hierarchy greatly appreciate your efforts. And now that you've completed your missions, all of you will be moving on.

"Our pagoda symbolizes change and change is about to come into your lives. As accredited Masters, your new assignments will be great spiritual gifts. May you enjoy them as the Light and Sound of our Eternal Maker guide you forward."

The ceremony finished, the Master of the Middle Universe bowed to his Co-Masters. Then he slowly walked toward a small park a short distance away. Once he reached one of its massive trees, he sat down and placed his back against its trunk. Then he crossed his legs. Now in the lotus position, he closed his eyes.

Seeing that the Master wanted to be left alone, Caraka smiled at his giant escort and said, "Well, we found the Master, but it looks as though he has other plans. I appreciate you bringing me here, but I think its time for me to go home. When you have a chance, can you please tell the Master that I stopped by? And that I'll return as soon as possible?"

Convinced that his short class in the pagoda was over, the Caraka placed his attention on his bed in his room and immediately transported himself there. The moment he arrived, his thoughts turned to the thirty foot beetle and the glitter it had in its aquamarine colored eyes when it had received its gift.

Who would have imagined that a pagoda symbolized change? Or that a giant beetle would appreciate receiving a miniature replica of a pagoda in recognition for all the spiritual work it had done in its lifetime.

But it had meant a great deal to that beetle.

*Masters of the Middle Universe receive crystal pagoda statues
as a tribute to their spiritual accomplishments and
the new assignments they're about to begin.*

9

The Rooster's Discourse

The Caraka stood up to close the door to his room. He was really tired and wanted to call it a day. However, before he could crawl in between the sheets he knew he had to visit the Master of the Inner Universe.

He collapsed into his favorite chair. Then he placed his attention on his third eye and projected himself to the temple where they always met. An instant later, he was in front of the crystal elevator looking around.

To his great joy, the spiritual conference was still in session. Countless Initiates of the Light and Sound were busy conversing with one another, while enjoying the event. Wondering if the Master was close by, the Caraka scanned the immense room for his tall body, but was unable to spot him.

Sensing the Master might be in the area where the initiates of his world normally met, he decided to go there. Fifteen Earth minutes later, he was within five hundred yards of the site and spied a large group surrounding the amphitheatre.

Wondering if something important was about to take place, he sped up until he reached the amphitheatre's main ramp. Then he looked down at the main stage and saw that they were all waiting for a speaker to begin a scheduled talk.

The speaker was at least thirty feet in height and greatly resembled a giant rooster. While the rooster stood in the center of the stage waiting to begin, the Caraka intuitively sensed it was important that he listen closely.

Then, with a gentle, loving, telepathic voice, the rooster called out for all to hear, "Thank you for attending this gathering. As most of you know I reside in a solar system located near the center of the physical plane.

"Our civilization consists mostly of roosters and hens such as myself. We are among the most ancient birds of the physical plane. The only thing we need in order to survive is the love of our Almighty Creator, and this is reflected by our level of consciousness.

"Our solar system and the three bordering it, are inhabited by the most advanced mammals, fish, birds, plants, reptiles, and insects found on the physical plane. We get along splendidly.

"Not too long ago, we came together to enjoy ourselves just as all of you are doing here. During this gathering, we were fortunate to be visited by a special Master from the fifth plane.

"This very advanced being was the principal speaker for the event and had previously lived on a nearby planet for hundreds of thousands of years. When he last lived among us, he was in the body of a woolly mammoth and was considered one of the most evolved Masters of the Middle Universe.

"We'd missed him greatly, and the moment he began his talk we listened closely to what he had to say. If you don't mind, I would like to share his words with you.

"With great love, he began, 'My beautiful friends. It is an immense pleasure to be among you again. As most of you know, I have been living on the fifth plane for a while now and am pleased to have finally adapted.

'Life is quite simple there. I routinely meet with the locals at the nearest amphitheatre to sing my love to God. When we finish,

I go wherever I want. But, I usually return to the small lagoon near my home. This is where I meet my closest friends.

'We bathe ourselves in the lagoon's pristine waters. Then we lie down to converse for hours and hours. If we run out of things to say, we travel to the small homes we have created for ourselves.

'At first, I thought I would get bored with this routine, but I was greatly mistaken. I never imagined how much I would enjoy getting together with the inhabitants of that world to talk about our lives and what we have learned.

'Everyone there is considered a Master, and we have much to share with each other. Fully activated, everyone of us can easily remember all of our past lives. Presently, I am learning so much about the worlds of God that it's impossible for me to get bored.

'Recently, I came to a startling realization. As my new friends and I share our stories, it feels as if a magic wand has been waved over us. Somehow, the pain and suffering we all went through while living in the lower planes has disappeared. Now, only the good from those difficult lives are remembered. Somehow, the negative memories have magically disappeared.' "

Shifting back and forth on its feet a number of times, the giant rooster stared out at the crowd, emitting massive amounts of love. Then it continued, "I greatly enjoyed the talk that my friend from the fifth plane gave, and a few hours later I spotted him in a corner of our temple by himself. Wanting to thank him for sharing his recent discovery with us, I walked over. Then I discovered he was crying.

"Caught completely off guard, I asked, 'Why are you crying old friend, your speech was beautiful?'

"Staring deeply into my concerned eyes, he replied, 'You might find this hard to believe, but I greatly miss living on the physical plane. I miss my friends and the love we shared with each other.

'Sure, I have new friends now. And I love them just as much. But I will never forget what my old friends and I went through while living in this world. A great paradox of the lower worlds has to do with love. Love exists everywhere, but while we are here we are normally too blind to recognize it.

'When one is finally able to see it all of the time, one's heart grows so much that it is overly sensitive. With this new sensitivity, pain has to be mastered in a different manner.'"

"After sharing this with me, I could tell that my friend was finished. He was ready to go home. He looked into my eyes one last time. Then he placed his attention on the fifth plane to return there.

"As his body slowly disappeared in the ethers of our temple, I began thinking about what he had just told me. I had never imagined that loving at a higher degree could be painful, but apparently it is.

"In conclusion, I would like to request something of you. I would like to request that each and every one of you make a greater effort to love your friends with all of your hearts. Once you do— be ready for the consequences. Because they will surely come."

Done with his speech, the Rooster walked off the stage and quickly blended into the crowd. As the Caraka watched his slight form disappear among the giant initiates of his current Master, the Caraka decided it was time for him to go home as well.

He placed his attention on his favorite chair and instantly projected himself there. The moment he opened his eyes, he shook his head in surprise. For so many years, he had been working hard to open his heart to share his love with others. But he had never considered the pain that might be incurred in the process.

Suddenly conscious of something very important, the Caraka realized he had to be more careful. From now on, he would do his best to include joy and happiness whenever he loved another being of God.

Because love always feels better when accompanied by other positive virtues of our Grand Creator.

When living in the higher worlds, negative memories magically disappear, while the good is remembered.

10

Arriving without Instructions

Turning off his computer, the Caraka walked over to the window of his room. It was early evening and he could see a full moon on the horizon. Knowing that Earth was on the outskirts of the physical universe, he wondered where the Middle Universe was positioned in respect to his little home.

Was it in front of him, behind him, above him, below him? And the Inner Universe, where was it located? Feeling lost without a map, the Caraka headed to his favorite chair, sat down, and closed his eyes.

Seconds later, he projected himself directly into the Master of the Middle Universe's Temple. Landing in front of the elevator, he quickly scanned the area, saddened to see that the enormous pilgrimage had come to an end. The attendees had returned to their homes.

Assuming the Master might be where his initiates gathered, he proceeded that way. But less than two hundred Earth yards away, he could tell that it was abandoned as well. He stopped to consider where they might be.

Moments later, his intuition told him that the Master was in the giant pagoda where he had handed out the statues. Hoping he was right, the Caraka quickly traversed the inner sanctum's glistening floor to find out.

When he passed through the pagoda's main entrance, he smiled to himself. The Master was sitting by himself in a special area set aside for contemplation. Eager to continue his inner world journey, the Caraka sat down at the Master's side to wait until he was finished.

When his mentor finally opened his eyes, the Caraka could see the heavenly bliss flowing through him. With an enormous grin, the Master gleefully called out, "Welcome little one. As you can see, our seminar has ended. Everyone has returned to their homes, and for the next few weeks I will be busy fulfilling the many promises I made to visit beings of the Light and Sound.

"As you arrived, I was visiting a planet on the border of the Inner and Outer Universes to meet with a large group of new initiates. Before I travel to the next site on my list, I would like to guide you to a very special place. Please climb onto my hand and I will take you there."

Slowly lowering his open palm, the Master watched closely as the Caraka climbed on. Then he closed his eyes. An instant later, the energy of the pagoda began to vibrate at a much higher rate.

Wondering where they were headed, the Caraka watched curiously as the two of them took off for a region of the physical plane he had never visited before. Twenty Earth seconds later, the Caraka saw that they were approaching what he could only describe as a central hub—a central hub connecting hundreds of galaxies. This unbelievably bright site resembled a giant ball of pinkish white light, and the Master steered him directly into its powerful energy.

Once through an even brighter off-white inner zone, the Master stopped and said, "Welcome little one. Welcome to the center of the physical universe. I brought you here for a special reason. Unbeknownst to the humans of your planet, a large number of the inhabitants of this site are your ancestors.

"Since the inception of the physical plane, they've been responsible for the spiritual development of your species, as well as mine. They are very advanced conduits of the Light and Sound-who have never taken a physical body.

"Still in the light bodies they accepted on the fifth plane eons ago, the only reason they're here is to create. There are hundreds of thousands of them, and I would like to introduce you to the Master assigned to watching over beings like you and me."

Caught completely off guard, the Caraka stared into his mentor's eyes in surprise. Then he looked out inquisitively as the two of them started moving again. An instant later, they stopped in the depths of the brilliant, off-white light.

Wondering what would happen next, the Caraka waited nervously. Then he spied a giant yellowish-white orb hundreds of Earth miles away. Sensing this might be the being the Master had mentioned, the Caraka stared at it in awe.

Then he heard a soft loving voice call out to him, "Hello old friend! I see you've brought a young student from the Outer Universe with you. Is this tiny being ready for the experience he is about to have?"

Lifting the Caraka high above his head, the Master joyfully replied, "Yes, he's ready. He's been training with the Ancient One and I felt it was time he meet you. Could you please tell him about the Inner Universe and how it came to be?"

Feeling the giant orb placing all its attention on him, the Caraka listened closely as it joyfully replied, "You have no idea how much I enjoy explaining how the physical universe was created and what my role was during that crucial cycle.

"Trillion of years ago, my friends and I were assigned to the fifth plane. We had been there for eons, enjoying ourselves in the Light and Sound of our Almighty Creator. Then, out of nowhere, a powerful blast of clear energy pushed the entire region where we lived into a black hole.

"With no idea where we were going, we watched and waited until we were eventually ejected out a far off portal. The moment we were on the other side, we realized that we had been transferred to a world of complete darkness.

"Quite surprised, we slowly took in our demanding surroundings. Then we clearly heard a voice from the tenth plane call out to us. It told us why we were there. To keep this inner-world experience simple, I will sum it up in one sentence. We were given the power to be Creators of God's energy in this dark void.

"At first we had no idea what we were doing. But eventually, we began imagining basic life forms such as stars and planets. Our world was slowly taking shape. As our assignment continued, we created smaller beings to inhabit these worlds. And the diversity of the physical plane slowly grew.

"After these beings, came multitudes of other life forms we knew nothing about. Fortunately, we had received ample training with the Light and Sound on the seventh plane. This training served us well and we quickly adapted to these unknown beings.

"As we did, we loved them greatly and they grew along with us. Right now, the physical plane is seventy percent created. It hasn't been easy, but we've done our best and will continue to do so for as long as we are here."

Caught off guard by this fantastic tale, the Caraka stared at his glimmering host. Then he had to ask, "If I heard correctly, God sent you here to create this world without any instructions? This doesn't sound like a good way to get things started?"

Finding the Caraka's observation humorous, the giant orb glimmered even more brightly as it replied, "Well, let me ask you a question. Did you come with instructions when you were born in your physical plane body? I don't think so.

"As far as I know, not one creature of the worlds of God comes with instructions. We are all given training before hand. And when the time comes, the Light and Sound of our Almighty Creator makes sure we get to where we need to go. It's that simple."

"Sometimes, we are placed in one of the giant rivers of energy that passes down from the higher worlds. At other times we are pushed through giant portals like we were. No matter how it happens, we all arrive where we need to be and give of ourselves for the good of the whole."

Suddenly aware that the orb's intense energy was overwhelming him, the Caraka knew he had to move back or suffer the consequences. Sensing his class might be over, he turned to the Master of the Middle Universe for guidance.

Seeing the enormous grin still on the Master's face, the Caraka watched as his mentor nodded his head up and down two times just as an Earthling would. Then he clearly heard his soft telepathic voice say, "Go home little one. Go home to your beautiful blue world."

Delighted to have met the giant orb, the Caraka immediately placed his attention on his room on planet Earth. When he opened his eyes an instant later, he remained seated in his chair for the longest time.

As he sat there, he reviewed the amazing conversation he had just had with the giant Orb Creator of the physical plane over and over. Especially the part about his birth.

Eventually, he had to admit that this immense being was right. He and every other inhabitant of the physical plane arrives without instructions. And as far as he knew, everyone seems to be getting along just fine.

*Every creature of God assigned to the lower worlds
arrives without instructions.*

11

Guided to the Egg-Shaped Temple

Feeling a little nervous, the Caraka walked over to his bed. This was to be his last class with the Master of the Middle Universe and he was anxious to find out where he would be going next. After sitting down, he leaned back against the headboard of his bed.

Comfortable, he slowly closed his eyes. An instant later he projected himself into the Master of the Middle Universe's temple. Arriving a short distance away from the area where the Master's initiates normally met, he spied his mentor meditating in the middle of the circular stage.

The Master was in a deep trance, so the Caraka silently sat down twenty yards away and placed his attention on his inner eye as well. Two Earth seconds later, he found himself being pulled into an orange wormhole.

On and on he traveled in this enormous passageway until a giant intersection appeared in the distance. With no idea where he was going, he was whisked down the right branch of the wormhole. Then the light around him instantly changed.

Now in a tunnel of yellowish-white light, the Caraka observed the glittering world passing by him. When he was finally pushed out of the passageway, he landed a short distance away from something greatly resembling a yellow cloud.

Rising high into the heavens above him, this enormous cloud looked just like any other cloud found on Earth—with two exceptions. Its enormous body was bright yellow in color. And its natural positioning was vertical instead of horizontal.

As he began to study this nebulous being, the soft voice of the Master of the Middle Universe called out, "Young Caraka, as you know our short time together has come to an end.

"In order to continue your inner-world training, the Ancient One requested that I guide you to this special site. The experiences you are about to have here will greatly alter your level of consciousness, allowing you to travel even higher into the worlds of our Almighty Creator.

"This 'cloud,' as you call it, might not look like much, but it is much more than you can imagine. Good-bye, my friend, until we meet again!"

Alone, the Caraka stared intently at the brilliant yellow energy before him. As far as he could tell, there was no entrance, nor any other distinguishing feature that warranted his attention. Only the giant egg-shaped formation of an enormous yellow cloud—that looked as if it were standing up.

Wondering if there was anyone nearby, he called out, "Hello, is there anybody here?"

Silence reigned, and the Caraka intuitively sensed that something was amiss. Remembering that it wasn't prudent to enter the space of giant spiritual beings without communicating with them first, the Caraka remained where he was and waited. And waited. And waited.

Finally he recognized that he needed help. He placed his attention on his beloved Master, the Ancient One. An instant later the image of this great being appeared in his inner eye and the Caraka asked, "Oh, Master, the Master of the Middle Universe guided me to a giant, yellow egg-shaped cloud. Can you please tell me what I'm supposed to do here?"

Wanting his student to continue this important inner-world journey, the Ancient One replied, "That enormous cloud happens to be the marker that everyone uses when they make the subtle transition from the sixth to the seventh planes.

"It's positioned strategically on the border between the two, and I would like you to project yourself directly into its egg shaped formation. Once inside, continue your journey to the super-giant temple in the center of the cloud.

"Look for its massive, oval entrance. Once you pass through it request an audience with the Master of the site. Tell this majestic being that I sent you there to begin your next eleven classes."

Certain the Caraka had enough information to continue this inner-world journey by himself, the Ancient One slowly faded away. Assuming he was about to meet his next mentor, the Caraka projected himself through the yellow cloud's thick outer membrane.

The instant he was on the other side he spotted a much brighter light in the distance. Certain he was heading toward the temple the Caraka continued his journey. When he was the equivalent of two Earth miles away, he recognized that the temple's light was so bright that it was the only object he could see.

It appeard to be an enormous egg-shaped mass. The Caraka stared at it until he found the temple's massive entrance. Remembering that the Ancient One had instructed him to pass through the entrance, the Caraka made a beeline for it.

Inside, he was astonished to find thousands upon thousands of skyscraper-type towers reaching high into the yellow ethers of the site. These towers reminded him of countless New York City Empire State Buildings, coming together to form one massive temple. Rising from the egg's center core, these buildings stopped half way to the site's outer egg shaped perimeter.

Wondering where he was supposed to announce himself, the Caraka continued observing this higher plane marvel until he saw a round, yellow light fly out from one of the towers.

This light appeared to be five or six hundred yards in diameter and the moment it reached him it stopped and called out, "Hello young traveler from the physical plane. I am the Master of this giant temple and cordially invite you to join me. You are now on the Alaya Lok and will be studying here for the next eleven classes.

"The energy of our world is quite soft, and I don't anticipate you having any trouble managing it. However, I advise you to keep in mind what you Earthlings call the Laws of the Universe whenever you visit our site. Only a handful of humans are aware that these laws were created here.

"A short distance away is the room where they were compiled and simplified for the countless beings living in the lower planes. These laws have been presented in various shapes and forms, first arriving on your blue planet more than five million years ago."

"In our temple, they consist of various shades of light. The best way to study them is to immerse yourself in their energy. For humans, these laws usually exist in shades of yellow and gold. They are considered crucial for the spiritual advancement of orb beings such as you.

"The instant a traveler of the Light and Sound finally immerses his essence in these noble hues, he will receive the knowledge needed to get past this point. I'm delighted you are here, young one, and look forward to working with you.

"When you feel you are ready to commence your training with me, please place your attention on the temple's entrance and pass through it just as you did this time. I will be nearby waiting for you."

Having formally received his new student, the Master of the Alaya Lok turned and headed for a giant plaza a short distance away. Then, the Caraka placed his attention on his room on planet Earth.

When he opened his eyes an instant later, he was happy to be in a world he knew so well. However tomorrow he would begin eleven classes in an enormous egg-shaped temple with Empire-State-Building-like spires. He hoped he was ready.

After merging with the yellow and golden energies of the Alaya Lok, spiritual travelers are allowed to continue training in the higher worlds above.

THE MASTER OF THE ALAYA LOK

12

Invited to the Master's Home

Returning home from work at the usual hour, the Caraka headed to his room. Throughout the day he had been thinking about the Alaya Lok and the new Master awaiting him there. Eager to begin his classes, he threw his backpack on his bed, removed his coat and sat down in his favorite chair.

As soon as he was comfortable, he closed his eyes and began concentrating on the entrance to the Temple of the Alaya Lok. Earth seconds later, he projected himself through it.

Remembering that the Master of the Alaya Lok had said he would be nearby, the Caraka cried out, "Hello Master, I've returned to begin my studies."

An instant later, his new mentor flew out of a nearby building.

When this great being was only a few feet away, it joyfully announced, "Welcome young seeker from the physical plane. Welcome to our world. For this class, I would like to give you a short tour of our temple so you will be better acquainted with the site."

Delighted with the invitation, the Caraka followed the Master as it quickly returned to the temple's vast plaza. In the plaza were millions of beings of the Light and Sound singing their love to the world around them. The Caraka suddenly felt compelled to join them.

Knowing it was impossible at the moment, he studied the brilliantly-lit plaza instead. Its flooring appeared to be of a golden crystalline material, while its outer perimeter was lined with hundreds of elongated egg-shaped towers, each rising high into the heavens.

When they reached the center of the plaza, the Master stopped and said, "This is where the inhabitants of our temple meet to participate in regularly-scheduled events. Right now, Souls of a pale yellow hue are here to sing their love to God. They are loving beings who belong to the same energy group you descend from.

"Most of them are ten feet in diameter and greatly enjoy giving of themselves. The instant they arrive, they merge with the love that permeates this site. Then they create their own love to share with others.

"The majority are here between assignments in the lower worlds and are scheduled to return shortly. Usually they go back and forth until they have mastered this constant exchange of God's precious energy wherever they happen to be. Now, I would like to show you where I live."

After making a beeline for the closest tower, the Master passed through its egg-shaped entrance, entering a brilliant aquamarine cabin that served as the building's elevator.

The Caraka felt absolutely no movement as he watched the floors of the building pass by. Earth seconds later, the elevator stopped and the Master led him through a triangular door.

He assumed this was the Master's home and slowly looked around. To his amazement, the circular room greatly resembled the inside of a giant multicolored basketball, illuminated by at least twenty different shimmering lights.

The Caraka counted thirty-three windows lining the room's outer walls. These enormous windows opened onto a panoramic view of the other buildings making up the gigantic temple.

More than impressed by the three-hundred-and-sixty degree view, the Caraka asked, "Is this where you spend most of your time?"

The Master replied, "Whenever I'm assigned to the seventh plane I stay here. As you can see, it has a breathtaking view. But the best thing about this place is that it allows me to be alone.

"Being a Master on any level is not easy. There are always countless seekers looking for guidance. Even though you do your best to help them, it never seems to be enough. If there were ten of me, my job would probably be easier. But there aren't.

"Please don't think I'm complaining, because I'm not. I greatly enjoy helping others and look forward to working with anyone that needs my assistance. However, my current assignment is constantly pushing me to be better than I am. This is never easy for anyone.

"Now, let's get started. The Ancient One asked me to work with you. Do you have any idea why?"

Staring blankly at the giant egg-shaped Master before him, the Caraka replied regretfully, "Well, no. I don't."

Eager to help his student grow spiritually, the Master's light shimmered brightly as it calmly replied, "You are here to learn how to give of yourself under every condition. What do you think of that?"

Aware he had to come up with a quick answer, the Caraka took a deep breath. Then he replied, "Well, I do my best to help others. But I know I can do better. Is there a secret one has to learn in order to do it right?"

The Master's light glowed even brighter as it answered, "Yes, there is a secret to learning how to give. And it has to do with your inner heart. Is your heart open enough to help others? Or is it just half open—only ready to give when it is convenient?"

Never having considered whether his heart was half or fully open, the Caraka candidly replied, "I don't know. How do I find out?"

His new mentor's light continued to glow brightly as it replied, "Well, I have an idea. Why don't you return to the plaza below us and mingle with a few of the beings there. Maybe one of them will help you find the answer to my question.

"Meanwhile, I'll remain here doing my spiritual exercise. I, too, need to connect myself with the holy essence of our Grand Creator as often as I can. It is the only way I can accomplish what I need to do. Please return to me when you have an answer."

The Caraka slowly retreated to the elevator leading to the plaza below them, re-entering its brilliant aquamarine light. When he reached the first floor, his thoughts turned to his assignment.

Somehow he had to find out if his heart was half open or whether it was fully open. How was he going to figure this out? Hoping for the best, the Caraka exited the Master's building and headed directly for the giant plaza.

As the Master had mentioned, the pale yellow orbs were still there. They were humming sacred words to themselves in deep contemplation. Quietly maneuvering himself around their glowing bodies, he recognized that they were concentrating so hard that they were unaware of his presence.

It was going to be hard to talk to one of them. He continued his silent walk into the group until he spied a small opening where he could observe them better. He stopped there and decided to join them in their contemplation.

With great joy in his heart he began concentrating on his inner essence, all the while humming a spiritual word that was very similar to theirs. Almost at once, the group's collective energy engulfed him.

Unsure whether he was sufficiently prepared to handle this energy, the Caraka kept humming his special word. Within five Earth minutes, he felt as if he had become a part of the group.

Thinking he could connect even better, he began giving more and more of himself to their collective energy. As he did he came to an important realization—the group needed him. For some reason, they needed his energy.

Wanting to contribute even more, he continued chanting. Then, during the final crescendo, the Caraka could have sworn that an invisible celestial conductor had waved its wand to end their magical melody.

The instant the pale-yellow orbs of this Alaya Lok chorus stopped singing, they took off for the many egg-shaped entrances of the towers surrounding the plaza as the Caraka watched incredulously.

He was the only one left in the plaza. Failing to discover whether his heart was open or not, he stared blankly out at the vast empty space around him.

Recognizing it was impossible for him to finish his first assignment on the Alaya Lok, he decided to forego his return to the Master's multicolored basketball home. Instead, he placed his attention on his own room on planet Earth.

Instantly he returned to the familiar surroundings of his comfortable home. Slowly opening his eyes, he absent-mindedly asked himself, "Is my heart open? Closed? Full? Half full? Three quarters full?"

He had no idea. The only thing he was certain of was that he was willing to do whatever was necessary in order to grow spiritually. And if he was doing something wrong, he knew the Master of the Alaya Lok would help him get it right.

Confident he would eventually come up with an answer, the Caraka went to prepare his evening meal.

Filling one's inner heart with the feeling of love is what every Soul must learn on the Alaya Lok.

13

Following the Pale Yellow Orb

He'd been sitting in his favorite chair for at least an hour. The Caraka knew it was impossible to stall any longer. He had to return to the Alaya Lok. He felt uncomfortable because he had failed to come up with an answer to the Master's question on his previous visit. But it was foolish to wait any longer. He placed his attention on his third eye and projected himself to the Alaya Lok.

The instant he arrived in the Master's enormous basketball-shaped home, he respectfully announced, "Hello Master, I've returned for my second class. Are you here?"

To his great joy, his new mentor cordially replied, "Hello, young one. How did it go in the plaza? Were you able to communicate with anyone?"

Aware he had failed his first assignment, the Caraka sheepishly replied, "Well, I was able to join the orbs singing there. But the moment they finished, they took off for the towers surrounding the plaza so fast that it was impossible for me to talk to anyone."

The Master's oval-shaped body began glowing brightly as it joyfully remarked, "I'm not surprised. Once those yellow beings complete their session, they evacuate the plaza as quickly as possible.

"Sometimes I think they learned this custom from former Earthlings. If I'm not mistaken, many of your workers punch time cards at the end of the day. Then they run away as fast as possible. If we placed a few of those machines and some time cards in the plaza, I'm certain we could reproduce that scenario perfectly."

Relieved that his new mentor was so accepting, the Caraka smiled and asked, "How am I supposed to communicate with one of them when they leave so fast?"

The Master continued glimmering as it calmly replied, "Well, why don't you follow one the next time. In fact, the same group should be there now."

Delighted to be given a second chance, the Caraka bolted for the cabin that led to the plaza. Moments later, he exited the Master's building and recognized the same orb-like beings he'd sung with during his last visit.

Hoping to communicate with one of them this time, the Caraka strolled in their midst until he found a spot to accommodate his small body. Then he began humming his sacred word in the same manner he had before.

Over and over, he sang this magical word until he felt his energy unite with the other orbs. He felt the love of God permeating his inner core as it had before. Sensing he was doing a good job, the Caraka thought this would be an excellent way to earn a living.

Getting together on a regular basis to share love with others was exhilarating. And once you were finished it appeared as if you could do whatever you wanted. If a profession of this type were ever offered on Earth, he was certain there would be long lines of humans applying for a position.

Finding this possibility a little humorous, the Caraka kept singing. Then, as on his previous visit, the celestial music came to a final crescendo. The moment it ended, he looked around at the many beings surrounding him.

He turned to the closest yellow orb and, before it could take off, the Caraka softly called out, "Can you please help me? I'm from another plane and would like to ask you a question."

Ignoring him completely, the orb made a beeline for a tower on the other side of the plaza. Watching incredulously, the Caraka realized that once again all the other orbs were doing the same thing. Within Earth seconds, he was the only one left in the plaza—again.

Desperate to communicate with anyone, the Caraka focused on the only remaining orb about to enter its tower. The Caraka took off in hot pursuit. But the moment he tried to pass through the entrance of its tower, he was repelled by an invisible security system.

It was impossible to go any further. The Caraka watched sadly as the last orb disappeared into the building's lobby. Feeling he had failed a second time, the Caraka slowly returned to the Master's tower, hoping he would be allowed to enter that site.

Before he entered however, it occurred to him that he didn't need entrances to get inside the buildings. As Soul, he could project himself anywhere he wanted. And if he wasn't mistaken, this meant he could track down any orb he wanted to.

Willing to give it a try, the Caraka stopped in front of the Master's building. Then he placed his attention on the yellow orb that had been singing at his side. An instant later, he found himself in an enormous room filled with thousands of Alaya Lok citizens immersing themselves in a giant pool of light pink liquid. The pale-yellow orb he had been tracking was soaking only a few yards away.

Anxious to complete the Master's assignment, the Caraka put as much love as he could in his tiny heart. Then he whispered to this fast moving chorus member, "Hello. I was singing next to you in the plaza and was wondering if I could ask you a question?"

Caught completely off guard, the orb looked up from the pool and replied, "Of course you can. What would you like to know?"

Thrilled to be finally communicating with a resident of this world, the Caraka continued, "Well, I'm from the physical plane. I just started taking classes with the Master of the Alaya Lok.

"On my last visit, the Master was explaining about the ability to give to others and asked me if I knew whether my heart was open or not. Unfortunately, I was unable to answer the question. Do you know anything about the subject?"

The pale yellow orb's light grew much brighter as it replied, "From what I can see, your heart is completely open at the moment. But this will probably change the moment you return to the physical plane.

"Lower-world schools are specifically set up to help beings learn how to give. I have spent many lifetimes there myself and am scheduled to return in a short while. My next assignment will be on the upper astral plane, and I'm delighted to be returning to that world."

Content to be learning about something he knew very little about, the Caraka queried, "How do you know you'll be returning to the upper astral plane?"

The Caraka's second question was just as easy to answer. The pale yellow orb replied, "On the fifth plane there is what you Earthlings would could call a special consul. It reviews our records through what could be considered a vast computer system, instantly analyzing our needs and the requirements of the worlds below us.

"The moment there's a match for the 'good of the whole,' the counsel is advised. Then it makes arrangements for us to live there. It's a very efficient system that has been in place for trillions of years."

Finding the orb quite informative, the Caraka asked a third question, "How were you able to tell that my heart is fully open?"

The yellow orb continued glowing brightly as it answered, "Well, that question is easy to answer as well. You wouldn't be here if your heart was half- or three-quarters open. Only beings that are a hundred percent open are allowed to journey to the seventh plane.

"On the physical plane, humans frequently have experiences that push them to extremes. When these experiences are of a negative nature, it is almost impossible for their hearts to stay open.

"However, if they learn to share their love with others, whether it be in a large group like ours, or on an individual basis, I can assure you that their hearts will remain open. This is the simplest solution to keeping one's heart open. If you are conscious of how it works, it will be almost impossible for you to fail."

He knew now that he had a good answer for the Master of the Alaya Lok. The Caraka smiled at his new acquaintance. Then he asked one last question, "Can I bathe in this pool? Or is only for the occupants of your tower?"

The pale-yellow orb chuckled as it explained, "There are many perks on the Alaya Lok, and sites such as this one are a good example. Everyone is welcome to use these pools whenever they want. I frequently do. After all, I'm about to return to the lower planes and I doubt I'll be as fortunate there."

With great appreciation for what the yellow orb had shared with him, the Caraka smiled at his new friend. Then he placed his attention on his home on the physical plane. Seconds later, he opened his eyes and grinned from ear to ear.

Happy to know that the Alaya Lok had beautiful pools awaiting him when he finally left Earth behind, the Caraka vowed to return there as often as possible. Declaring his love to his Almighty Creator while soaking in the divine nectar of the Alaya Lok was something an Earthling like him could really look forward to.

Living on the Alaya Lok requires that a being of the Light and Sound maintain its heart open to love at all times.

14

Another Question

Delighted to be home from work, the Caraka climbed the steps to his room two at a time. He was in a hurry to return to the Alaya Lok, and the instant he closed the door behind him, he plopped down in his favorite chair.

More relaxed than on his previous visit, he gazed into his third eye. Then, with very little effort, he projected himself into his new mentor's giant basketball-shaped room, anxious to answer the Master's question. But the room was empty.

Hoping to find his mentor in the plaza, he raced to the elevator. The instant he exited the building he spotted another group gleefully singing their love to the world around them. These beings however, were much different than the ones he had sung with on his previous visit.

They resembled giant eggs—giant eggs lying down on their sides. Each egg appeared to be close to three hundred yards in length and as he carefully examined their immense bodies he wondered where they were from.

Because of their enormous proportions, the plaza could not hold as many of them. Estimating their number at about twenty thousand, he questioned the roles they played in the worlds of God.

Sensing they wanted to be left alone, the Caraka did his best to silence his loud thoughts as he continued to observe them from the entrance to the Master's building. Then he resumed his search for his teacher.

Very slowly, he followed the plaza's outer perimeter until he eventually returned to the Master's tower. His teacher had to be somewhere close by. The Caraka placed his attention on his inner eye to continue his search.

Clearly visualizing the Master a few Earth seconds later, he traversed the outer wall of the plaza's tallest tower, letting his mentor's energy guide him to where it was.

Inside, he could see that he had entered a vast oval-shaped room. In the middle of this room was the Master of the Alaya Lok conversing with a group of initiates of the Light and Sound of all shapes and sizes.

Pleased to see his student, the Master called out, "Welcome, little one. I sensed your presence in the plaza and decided to wait for you until you tracked me down."

Grateful that it had been so easy, the Caraka smiled while silently observing the Master's friends. A few of them were medium-sized orbs, while a large number were egg-shaped beings.

Seven resembled large hexagons, and he realized this was the first time he had ever seen six-sided beings. A few were his size, but most of them were much larger. At least thirty were smaller egg-shaped beings. He wondered where they all came from.

Suddenly afraid he had barged in on their meeting, the Caraka timidly asked, "Am I interrupting something important?"

The Master's pale yellow light began glimmering brighter than usual as it joyfully replied, "No, you aren't interrupting anything. In fact, you arrived just in time. We've been discussing an interesting subject, and I would like you to give us your opinion.

"Do you think it is easy for beings of the Light and Sound to learn how to travel to the higher worlds while residing in the lower planes?"

Amazed that these beings would want to know what he thought, the Caraka blinked a few times in surprise. Then he replied, "Well, I can only tell you what happened to me. I was completely unaware of my abilities as Soul until a friend gave me a book that discussed the art of traveling in the inner worlds.

"It took a little more than six months, but once I figured out how to do it, it became second nature to me. I could leave my body whenever I wanted. The key was accepting that I had the capacity to travel in the inner worlds. Once I got past that hurdle, everything came naturally."

Appreciating the Caraka's concise reply, the Master smiled at the diverse group surrounding him. Then he continued, "This student from the physical plane seems to think that the hardest part was accepting that he could do it. Now I'm curious what you Masters from the other areas of the lower worlds think?"

Not at all bashful, a giant egg shaped Master began to shimmer brightly as it declared, "We recently determined that when a civilization is at peace, its inhabitants have a better chance of opening themselves to the teaching of the Light and Sound. Wars, or extreme feelings of anger or hatred, block the love of God."

Enjoying the exchange of information, the Master of the Alaya Lok quickly added, "Yes, peace and harmony are always important. But in many regions of the lower worlds they are nonexistent. In these areas, it is important we do our part to get the word out, no matter how difficult it might be.

"As you just heard from our visitor from Earth, it wasn't difficult for him to figure how to travel in the inner worlds, once he discovered he could do it. If we step up our efforts to get this information out, I'm sure an infinite number of seekers will come to the same conclusion."

Grateful the Caraka had arrived at just the right moment to participate in his class, the Master turned to him and said, "Thank you for tracking me down. Your input is greatly appreciated. But now we must continue our discussion without you."

Astounded and honored to have made a contribution, the Caraka smiled at the beings surrounding him. Then he placed his attention on his room on the physical plane. Seconds later he opened his eyes and began shaking his head in disbelief.

Who would have thought that after plopping down into his chair and closing his eyes, he would join the Master of the Alaya Lok as he convened with a number of other Masters of the Lower Worlds.

His intention had been to answer the question he had failed to answer in his first class. Instead, he found himself in front of a group of very advanced beings, answering a different question. Fortunately, it had been an easy one.

If this was what his inner-world journeys to the Alaya Lok were going to be like, he had to be better prepared. The Alaya Lok was all about giving, and if he was going to be asked to give verbally, he wanted to have some idea of what he was talking about.

The most difficult hurdle for inner-world travelers
is accepting they can do it.

15

Conversing with a Creator

Feeling inexplicably anxious, the Caraka sat down on his bed. Something important was about to happen—he could feel it. Assuming it would take place on the Alaya Lok, he propped up his pillow behind his head. Then he stilled his senses.

Doing his best to remain calm, he closed his eyes and began searching for his new mentor. Seconds later, he located the Master at the entrance of its giant skyscraper home, patiently waiting for him.

When he was a few feet away, the Master called out, "Young Caraka, for this inner-world journey I would like to guide you to one of my favorite sites. It's on the Upper Alaya Lok. Are you ready?"

Before the Caraka could even reply, the Master began enveloping him with its loving energy. He watched curiously as his tiny essence was pushed into a golden wormhole. Three Earth seconds later, the Caraka emerged in a region of the seventh plane he had never visited before.

As he approached something that greatly resembled an enormous white pillow standing up on end, the Caraka wondered what it could be. This enormous pillow appeared to be larger than the Milky Way Galaxy. The instant they reached its cloud-like perimeter, the Master abruptly stopped.

Then the Master courteously explained, "We're on the border of the eighth plane, known as the Hukikat Lok. This enormous white being may resemble a giant pillow to you, but I wouldn't recommend attempting to lie on it. I myself have never gone any closer than where we are now."

Curious, the Caraka queried, "Why can't you go any closer?"

The Master's white light seemed to dim as it replied, "This giant being is the Grand Creator for the seventh plane. Whatever it thinks, comes to pass.

"However, it doesn't think in the same manner that you or I do. This being's role in the worlds of God forces it to think on a much higher level, a level so high that it is considered one of the nine supreme Creators of God."

Remembering that this was one of the Master's favorite places to visit, the Caraka asked, "Why do you like coming here if you can only go this far?"

The Master's loving energy passed through him strongly as it answered, "Have patience little one. The site I visit is nearby."

Moments later the Caraka felt himself being directed upward. When they began to slow down, he realized that the Master was steering him to what he could only describe as a nest on top of the pillow.

In the middle of this nest was a giant egg-shaped temple that greatly resembled the temple where the Master lived. It had a giant plaza as well, with tall skyscraper towers surrounding it. Seemingly in a hurry, the Master guided him to a large white altar in the middle of the plaza.

Then the Master said, "This altar is connected to the massive pillow-shaped being below us. It serves as its communication center. From this site all its thoughts and creations are emitted to the world around us. Fortunately, the altar's energy is calibrated to allow inner-world travelers such as you to approach it. Do you have any questions for this amazing being?"

Humbled to be visiting one of the main Creators of God, the Caraka nervously asked, "What is the difference between a Master of the Light and Sound and a Creator such as this white cloud?"

The altar's light began to glimmer brightly as it replied, "Your question is one that only a young traveler from the physical plane would ask. Let me explain.

"On the physical plane, Masters are very common. But Creators of a plane are unknown. Few Earthlings of your blue world are aware that enormous beings like me even exist. For this reason, I will try to enlighten you as to what we do.

"Masters, such as the ones you have been studying with, do their best to teach their students about God, love, and the basic laws to be followed in order to reach their eternal home.

"A Creator such as myself, emits the energies needed to make sure that the worlds of God are alive and well. This signifies, for example, that the Creator of the physical plane interacts with larger beings such as your Milky Way Galaxy to guarantee it has everything its needs to survive.

"A Master does its best to guide aspiring Souls back to their true home. A Creator does its best to keep the larger beings of God functioning as they should."

Astonished to be conversing with a being with so much responsibility, the Caraka replied, "I know what a galaxy is. And now, I have a vague idea of what the Creator of the physical plane does. However, I know very little about the Alaya Lok and the beings that live here. Can you tell me who you work with on this plane?"

The altar's powerful pale yellow light began to expand. Before the Caraka could react, he found himself flying through the ethers of the seventh plane at an amazing velocity.

As he traveled on, the Creator of the Alaya Lok continued, "Look around you and tell me what you see."

Moving so fast he could barely scan the world around him, the Caraka did his best to glimpse the zone of the Alaya Lok he was passing through. Earth-seconds later, he realized he was flying through a zone filled with countless white pillowed-shaped beings.

Impressed by their beauty, he softly replied, "Well, it looks as if there are billions upon billions of white pillow-shaped beings that greatly resemble the cloud under the city where your altar is located."

As he began to see them much more clearly, he continued, "Recently the astronomers of my planet have been taking a lot of telescopic photos. These beings resemble the countless galaxies that exist on the physical plane."

Pleased with the Caraka's observation, the Creator of the Alaya Lok responded, "You're right. These billions upon billions of white pillows, as you call them, are the equivalent of the galaxies of your world.

"I'm responsible for making sure they are functioning as they should. In the center of the physical plane exists a highly-charged area where the Creator of your world resides. And it does virtually the same thing I do here."

Astonished to be learning about the responsibilities of a Creator of God, the Caraka continued scanning the site. Then he asked a final question, "Can you please tell me why God has all of us scattered all over the place? From what I've been told, life was pretty good for everyone before the lower worlds were created."

Amused by the Caraka's question, the Creator of the Alaya Lok joyfully replied, "The reason the worlds of God were altered has to do with creativity and allowing the offspring of our Almighty Creator the opportunity to create for themselves.

"God itself did not need this expansion, but its little children did. For this reason, the worlds of duality were created.

"Over the years, I have worked with all the Creators of the lower planes and can assure you that they are doing exactly what our Almighty Creator requested of them. They are slowly expanding their worlds in order to bring needed experiences to the children of the Light and Sound training there.

"Similar to a city on planet Earth that is in the process of growing, the worlds of God are creating suburbs for the many Souls that are being relocated there. Your physical plane happens to be one of the farthest suburbs at the moment, but eventually this will change."

Aware that they were discussing things way beyond his capacity to understand, the Caraka took a deep breath and decided to forego any further questions. At this point he was just delighted to be able to understand the Creator of the Alaya Lok's simple explanation. But deep inside he sensed this creative process was much more complicated.

Hearing the Caraka's loud thoughts, the Creator of the Alaya Lok continued, "I've given you a simple but concise explanation of what my co-Creators and I do and how this elaborate system came to be.

"As you continue your inner-world journeys, your level of consciousness will adjust to compensate for your ever-growing vision of the worlds we all live in. As you grow, you will have to continue equating enormous beings of God to large, white pillows and anything else that facilitates your comprehension of the ever-expanding planes we are constantly creating. In fact, your next class will bring you another small piece of this giant puzzle. Until we meet again, little one."

Clearly his class with this amazing being had come to an end. The Caraka lovingly gazed at the billions upon billions of white pillow-type beings surrounding him. Then he placed his attention on his home on planet Earth.

The moment he opened his eyes he grabbed the pillow he had been leaning against and held it up in front of him. As he stared at its familiar shape, he shook his head in disbelief.

Who would have thought that all over the worlds of God were enormous Creators that looked just like his pillow, making certain that everything was functioning as their Almighty Creator had envisioned everything to be.

The worlds of God are constantly creating suburbs for the countless Souls routinely assigned there.

16

Blinded by the Brilliant White Altar

Racing up the steps to his room two at a time, the Caraka collapsed into his favorite chair. He just *had* to return to the Alaya Lok. Feeling almost obsessed, he placed his attention on his third eye and projected himself into the Master of the Alaya Lok's basketball-shaped room.

An instant later he spied the Master seated in front of one of the windows of the room. It appeared that the Master was meditating. With little desire to disturb him, the Caraka sat down a few feet away and placed his attention on his inner eye as well.

A split second later, he found himself approaching what he could only describe as a large ocean of pale yellow light. This massive body of energy sprawled out in every direction. He wondered where it was located in the higher worlds.

Certain the Master had guided him there for a reason, the Caraka decided to explore this massive body of yellow light. Traveling upward in an ever growing spiral he flew countless Earth miles until he spied a small island in the distance. Sensing it was a site of importance, he made a beeline for it.

When he was almost upon it, he realized he had made a mistake. The island wasn't small at all. It was enormous and shaped in the form of a great heptagon. He saw off-white pyramids dotting its smooth terrain. Assuming the pyramids housed the inhabitants of this world, he concluded that the island was heavily populated.

His curiosity piqued, the Caraka continued his journey until he spied a pale yellow altar on the horizon. Almost certain this was where the Master wanted him to go, he took off in its direction.

Soon the altar's light was too intense to go any further. He stopped. Finding it impossible to look into its brilliant energy, he quickly realized that it might knock him out of balance.

Wanting to avoid this, the Caraka quickly spun around to study the landscape behind him. He was delighted he had, for all around the altar were giant, tree-like beings he had failed to see on the way in. Off-white in color, these trees formed what had to be the largest forest he had ever seen in the inner worlds.

Impressed by this extraordinary site, the Caraka listened closely as the Master of the Alaya Lok's soft telepathic voice called out, "Young traveler, thank you for allowing me to continue my inner-world voyage uninterrupted.

"I was in the middle of a conversation with a Master from another plane, and it was impossible for me to give you my full attention. However, this did not prohibit me from guiding you to this important site.

"The altar behind you is the most powerful being on the Alaya Lok. As you have already discovered, its energy must be respected. I am pleased you were able to recognize the power it wields before you went any further! It is aware you have traveled here from the physical plane and would like to converse with you. I will leave you in its good company."

Having done its part, the Master's soft energy instantly faded away.

To comply with his new mentor's request, the Caraka slowly turned to meet this powerful being. Still blinded by its brilliant off white light, the Caraka squinted as he called out, "Hello, white altar. You are one of the brightest objects I've been guided to in the worlds of God. Are you like this all of the time?"

The altar's light suddenly grew brighter as its soft telepathic voice replied, "My energy is like this most of the time. However, every now and then I get a request to raise the energy of the worlds below me. When this happens I get much, much brighter. During these concentrated cycles it would be foolish for any orb-like being, such as you, to be anywhere near me."

Curious, the Caraka queried, "What kind of situation would require this type of action on your part?"

The off-white altar's energy remained constant as it replied, "The Master of the Alaya Lok was right, you do ask a lot of questions.

"What kind of situation requires this type of energy? Well, I'm not sure if your current level of consciousness will permit you to comprehend what I am about to say. But it's worth a try.

"My energy is important whenever a black hole of the lower planes needs energy to fulfill its mission. I'm not sure if you are aware of this, but these important beings require enormous quantities of energy in order to fulfill their missions.

"In order to obtain this energy, they pull it from the world immediately above them. Once they have enough, they transfer it to the planes below them. Serving the same function as an enormous funnel, they pass life on to where it is most needed.

"When I first began my mission I had to create giant rivers of pale yellow light and direct their energy to the black holes that exist at the bottom of the fifth plane. This action was taken in order to feed the new plane being created there.

"Once that world was capable of existing on its own, I created more rivers to feed the black holes existing below that plane. Now, these planes have been functioning perfectly for billions of Earth years, and I'm pleased to say that all is well.

"At this moment, black-hole activity has increased on the lower astral and lower physical planes. They are assisting the Creators of those worlds put in place according to what was envisioned eons ago.

"When the physical plane finally becomes the school it was meant to be, I will stop sending my energy to the black holes of the lower astral plane and divert it to the newly created black holes feeding the dark plane below the world you currently live on.

"In this slow, but efficient manner, the Universities of God are continuing to grow, with the goal of accommodating us all. This is my way of being a Co-worker with our Almighty Creator."

Pleased to be conversing with this amazing being, the Caraka just had to ask, "What happens to your energy once the black holes send it to the worlds below them?"

Anticipating the question, the altar softly replied, "Once a black hole pushes the energy I've sent to the plane below it, it creates a number of "Big Bang" type waves that emanate in every direction.

Fortunately, my energy is DNA-coded and is able to create the various life forms that are destined for that world. As you recently learned, every plane is different due to the assignments given to the Creators that are willing it to life.

"As this precious work continues, the level of consciousness of the lower worlds will slowly rise. Eventually, this will allow the planes closest to the higher worlds to be absorbed into them."

Having finished its explanation, the white altar fell silent.

Grateful for this astonishing information, the Caraka smiled joyfully as he said, "Thank you for explaining this complicated process to me. I'm amazed at how everything is being slowly put into place.

"However, I need some time to think it through. If there is something I don't understand, can I come back to visit you some other time?"

Pleased with the Caraka's request, the altar began to glow more brightly as it replied, "Of course you can! But be sure to approach me only when my energy is as it is now."

Certain that this interesting class had come to an end, the Caraka made one last attempt to peek in the altar's direction. Concluding it was still impossible to look directly at it, he decided to go home instead.

He placed his attention on his precious blue world and projected himself there. When he opened his eyes a few seconds later, he was delighted to see his planet's bright yellow sun.

It was clearly visible as it slowly settled over the mountains on the other side of the valley. It, too, was too bright for him to look at directly and he wisely turned his head. Comparing it to the off-white altar he had just conversed with, the energy of Earth's sun was minuscule.

Nevertheless, it was enough to keep him and every living being on his blue world alive and well. And that was all that mattered to the multiple life forms lucky enough to be here.

Black holes serve as giant funnels, passing the energy of life to wherever it is needed most.

17

Replenishing the Eternal Sponge

Staring at his tired face in the bathroom mirror, the Caraka saw how exhausted he was. It had been a long day. Now only his spiritual exercises stood between him and a good night's sleep. Hoping to finish his class as quickly as possible, he collapsed into his favorite chair and closed his eyes.

He placed his attention on the Master of the Alaya Lok's home. An instant later, he stood scanning his current mentor's room. The Master wasn't there. Wanting to continue his class he began concentrating on its energy.

Milliseconds later, he found himself less than two miles from a giant, yellow cascade. Astonished by the size of this immense falls, he watched as its pristine liquid flowed slowly past him.

Finding it impossible to see the falls outer perimeter, the Caraka suddenly felt himself being pulled toward its slowly moving energy. When he was less than twenty yards way, he was surprised to see the Master bathing in its yellow liquid. The Caraka couldn't help but chuckle to himself.

Delighted that the Caraka had arrived, the Master called out, "Welcome, young one. This magical cascade happens to be where six rivers merge to form one of the major sources of the Light and Sound.

"All six rivers originate on planes above us, and from this point on their combined energy continues to nourish the many worlds below. I frequently come here to immerse myself in its precious liquid. It has a soothing affect on my body, and I recommend it to anyone who wants to unwind. Why don't you join me?"

The timing was perfect. The Caraka took a few steps forward. Then he sidled up to the Master and watched as the river's yellow energy continued flowing around the two of them.

Before he could ask one of his many questions, the Master added, "At least fifty percent of this energy comes from the Agam Lok, or the ninth plane of God. It continues in this state to the fifth plane. Very little of it will be dispersed on the Alaya Lok."

"Brimming with pure love, a tiny portion of this immense river is destined to nourish a sub-plane of the physical plane below the one you currently reside on. This plane is relatively new and was created for the beings of the Middle and Outer Universes who failed to put into practice the Laws of our Almighty Creator in previous incarnations."

Surprised to learn that this massive river was going so far, the Caraka continued to stare absent-mindedly into its yellow light. As it slowly flowed past him, its soft energy soothed him. Feeling more relaxed than when he had arrived, he remembered that this often happened whenever he visited magical sites.

Wondering how this process worked, the Caraka asked, "Dear Master, as you stated, the river's energy is helping me relax. This often occurs whenever I visit special sites during inner-world journeys. Can you please explain why the Light and Sound of far off sites such as this have the capacity to help me while I'm still living in a physical body?"

Delighted with the Caraka's question, the Master's light suddenly grew brighter. It joyfully replied, "You are a being of love, and your eternal essence consists of the Light and Sound. The moment you joined me here in the river, your inner core instinctively absorbed as much of the energy passing by us as you needed. Without your being aware, you began replenishing the light you lack.

"As a small orb, or Soul, originally from the higher worlds, you are the equivalent of a sponge—a round sponge who once was brimming with the essence of love. After a few assignments on the outskirts of the physical plane, this love has greatly diminished.

"Only a reduced amount of the Light and Sound remains in your inner essence. As Soul, you are aware that you are losing this energy. And your eternal core is desperately seeking the love you've lost.

"Frequently, you can rekindle this love through a mate or cherished family member. At other times, you are able to replenish it with a pet or close friend. If you happen to be a conscious being of the Light and Sound, you might be led to one of the powerful chakras of your planet to refill yourself.

"There are many ways to re-supply your sponge-like core with the energy it needs, but you must make an effort to find it. A river such as this is a fantastic way to receive the essence of the higher worlds. I frequently come here to replenish my inner being."

Delighted that he understood what the Master was telling him, the Caraka calmly studied the cascade's yellow energy as it continued flowing past him. He had never thought about it before, but now that the Master had mentioned it, he agreed. He was a sponge—a small sponge constantly doing its best to replenish itself with the love of God.

It was easiest when he was around beings who returned his love. Or when he traveled to special sites that radiated beautiful energy—such as a majestic mountain or ocean. But there were other times when he found it very difficult to share his love with anyone.

To make matters worse, he sometimes ended up in areas that seemed to suck the energy out of him instead of replenishing him. During these unexpected visits, he had had to rely on his connection with his Inner Master to pull himself up.

Suddenly remembering something important, he turned to face the Master of the Alaya Lok and asked, "I often travel into the higher worlds to fill myself with love. I visit special sites, such as this one, just to get by on the physical plane.

"I was wondering, is it imperative that I fill myself with the love found on planet Earth? Or is okay for me to merge with the love I find in the higher worlds to compensate for what I'm lacking?"

Pleased with the Caraka's question, the Master replied, "Love is love, no matter where you come across it."

Not at all surprised by the Master's concise answer, the Caraka continued staring at the bright yellow liquid of love flowing past him. Then he just had to shout, "Thank you, beautiful energy of God's love. Thank you for helping me keep my inner sponge filled with your beautiful essence."

Knowing his class was over, he placed his attention on his room and instantly projected himself there. When he opened his eyes a few seconds later, he felt ecstatic to have visited that magical site.

Still enjoying the river's restorative energy pulsating throughout his entire body, he couldn't help but feel great. Knowing it would be difficult for him to fall asleep anytime soon, he remained seated in his favorite chair for the longest time, smiling to the silent world around him.

Our eternal essence, or Soul, is constantly looking to replenish the love of God lost after many reincarnations on the lower planes.

18

Guided to an Ancient Relative

Reflecting joyfully on his inner-world classes on the Alaya Lok, the Caraka closed his eyes. When he felt completely relaxed, he placed his attention on his new mentor's energy and quickly headed toward it.

Within milliseconds, he spotted the Master hovering a short distance from a giant orb. This white orb appeared to be millions of times larger than the sun that warmed his blue planet. He wondered why the Master had guided him there.

Eagerly, he continued onward, until he was less than ten yards away. "Hello Master," he called out. "I'm here for my next class. Is there anything you would like me to do?"

Delighted the Caraka had arrived, the Master's light grew much brighter. Then it replied, "Welcome young one. Welcome to a very special site. We are on the vast border of the seventh and eighth planes once again, home to this enormous being of the Light and Sound.

"During your many inner-world journeys you've been introduced to a number of giant orbs, all of which play important roles in the spiritual hierarchy of our Grand Creator. But none are comparable to this great being."

Curiosity piqued, the Caraka shifted his gaze to the giant white globe before him.

He listened closely as the Master continued, "This giant is in direct contact with the energy source you call God. It serves as God's communication center from the seventh plane down.

"Whenever the Energy of God decides to do something below this site, it informs this white orb to get everything going. It could be considered one of God's executive assistants, and its role is vital as the planes below us continue their steady expansion."

Surprised, the Caraka focused on the enormous orb before him. As he calmly scanned it, he realized that he was being slowly pulled into its energy. He finally came to a stop, astonished to find himself floating in the middle of the orb's glimmering white light.

Feeling a little out of place, the Caraka wondered what was going to happen next. But nothing happened. Silence reigned in this brilliant white world.

Sensing he should communicate with this powerful being, the Caraka softly whispered, "Your energy began pulling me into your body the moment the Master of the Alaya Lok informed me about the role you play in the worlds of our Grand Creator. So far I feel pretty good here, and I hope this continues. Can you please tell me why the Master guided me to you?"

The equivalent of two Earth seconds later, the barely perceptible voice of the giant orb replied, "Welcome, young one. Welcome to my white domain. You are visiting me for a very simple reason. Humans of planet Earth know very little about the worlds of our Grand Creator.

"In order to change this, the Ancient One requested that you be introduced to a number of the bigger beings of the higher worlds. He also asked that we give you some basic information on what we do.

"Once you finish your classes with us, we expect you to share what you learn with others. This way Earthlings will have a better idea of what awaits them once they leave their blue planet behind.

"God is not an old man with long white hair, but rather the combined energy of a number of higher-world beings. Their energy consists of different degrees of love. The beautiful melodies expressing their love are constantly flowing to the realms they've created in the form of the Light and Sound.

"Just like any white cloud floating in your light blue sky, my white energy might appear to be insignificant. But I can assure you that amazing events are taking place within my precious body. During this visit, you should consider yourself a tourist—a tourist fortunate to have been allowed to experience a number of my magical sites."

Sensing this inner-world voyage was going to push him to his limits, the Caraka wondered if he was ready. Then the orb's energy began to change. An instant later, he recognized that he had been transported to an area of clear light.

This immense area appeared to be super-charged with electricity. As he quickly took in its powerful energy, he could see something like tiny embers flickering on and off all around him.

Standing in the middle of this impressive light show, he listened closely as the white orb's soft telepathic voice continued, "The energy around you can be compared to the fastest computer ever built on your planet. It communicates the desires of our Grand Creator to the worlds below and can see, hear, feel, and do a number of other things humans know nothing about.

"Now, I will guide you to another of my precious sites. This time the Caraka found himself approaching what he could only describe as a swirling ball of white light. This light flowed in a clockwise direction and as the Caraka drew close to its perimeter, he recognized it as a giant Super-Soul.

Quite impressed, he studied the swirling ball's essence as the giant white orb continued, "You're right little one. You are in the presence of a giant Super-Soul—a Super-Soul in direct contact with the Creators of each plane.

"Its mission is to put into motion the thoughts and feeling of our Almighty Creator. It instantly relays any instructions coming from above. This will probably surprise you, but the humans of your world are tiny offspring of this grand being. Because of this relationship, you have been gifted with the capacity to create as well.

"Unbeknownst to Earthlings, humanoid Souls are found throughout the worlds below us. They are magnificent receptors of the Light and Sound, actively contributing to the advancement of our Grand Creator's love, thoughts and feelings. This is why little orb beings like you are cherished beyond belief."

Honored to be related to this majestic Super-Soul, the Caraka pondered what this meant to him. For years he had been traveling in the inner worlds and had never come across a super-being that was at all similar to him until now.

Still not completely convinced, the Caraka asked, "Are you saying that I'm kind of a tiny replica of this giant mass of swirling energy?"

Pleased the Caraka wanted more information, the giant white orb replied, "Of course you are. All orbs, or Souls, are originally born in the massive Ocean of Love and Joy of the Anami Lok— the tenth plane. Once created, they are assigned to the many worlds of our Grand Creator.

"Depending upon the epoch in which they were created, they are grouped into distinct categories. Some were inducted into the Order of the Orbs, while others were inducted into the Order of the Souls of the Light and Sound. There are fifty five different categories in total, and you will slowly learn about them as you complete your inner-world journeys."

Amazed to be in the presence of this ancient being, the Caraka stared into its powerful energy. As he did, the white orb softly whispered, "Your tour with me is over. But, whenever you have some free time, I invite you to return here to learn more about my amazing world."

Before he could thank his giant host for the incredible tour, the Caraka was expelled from its white light. Knowing his class was over for the day, the Caraka placed his attention on his bedroom on planet Earth and instantly transported himself there.

When he opened his eyes, he found it impossible to think about anything but the giant Super Soul he had met. After all, he was related to it somehow. He might even be able to consider it his grand, grand, grand, infinitely grand, grandfather!

Every being ever created has ancient relatives waiting for them throughout the higher worlds.

19

The Donut City

Walking to the window of his room, the Caraka gazed out at his quiet neighborhood. His recent inner-world journeys were greatly altering him, and he wondered if he was adapting quickly enough.

Knowing that his beloved Master, the Ancient One, was monitoring his every move, he was fairly certain he wasn't going too far, too fast. But deep inside, he had his doubts and hoped he could keep up the demanding pace.

Confident the Ancient One would stop him if he was being pushed beyond his limits, he returned to his favorite chair and sat down. Then he closed his eyes and placed his attention on the Master of the Alaya Lok.

The equivalent of two Earth seconds later, he spied his new mentor on the banks of an enormous river of yellow light, watching the river's energy as it flowed in a downward direction.

Wondering why he was there, the Caraka closed the gap between them and softly called out, "I'm here for my next class. Is this river connected to it somehow?"

The Master's light began glowing brightly as it cheerfully replied, "Yes it is. If you don't mind, I would like you to jump into the river. Let its yellow energy guide you to the beautiful city downstream. This city is one of the most important sites of the

Alaya Lok and a must for you to experience."

Delighted to comply with the Master's simple request, the Caraka jumped into the river and began flowing along with it. He was surprised to discover that the river consisted of a fluffy type of energy—energy that made it impossible for him to sink.

Content to be floating on top of its downy essence, the Caraka traveled at an amazingly fast rate. After the equivalent of twenty thousand Earth miles, the river curved around a big sweeping bend, approaching what the Caraka could only describe as a giant donut of bluish-white light. He did his best to see what lay ahead.

In the distance, the river appeared to be flowing directly through the center of the massive donut. Intuitively sensing this must be the city the Master had mentioned, the Caraka took a deep breath, hoping he was ready for this inner-world experience.

The instant his tiny body reached the donut's enormous center, he was plucked off the river's surface. Floating in the ethers of the magical site, the Caraka looked around with curiosity as he was propelled to the city's main plaza.

When he alit in the middle of the circular site, he was surprised to find himself standing in front of a giant monument resembling a donut. Knowing there had to be a good reason why the Master had sent him there, the Caraka began to examine the enormous object.

As he did, vast amounts of intense energy slowly passed through him. Concerned that it might be too strong for him, he backed off a few paces and continued studying the world around him.

During a previous inner-world class, he had discovered that obelisks were important transmitters of God's energy. But he had never before encountered a donut that was capable of doing the same thing. In order to confirm this, the Caraka cautiously advanced toward the enormous monument.

When he was a short distance away, he called out, "The Master of the Alaya Lok requested that I travel in the river until I reached this site. Would you happen to know why the Master sent me here?"

The giant donut's bluish-white light began sparkling brightly as it replied, "Your current mentor and I are good friends, and it informed me you were on the way. Since you currently reside on the physical plane, it is important that you take great care while you are here. A few areas of our magical city are so powerful that they could easily dismantle your inner core."

Greatly concerned, the Caraka stopped in his tracks. Then he asked, "Why is your donut energy so powerful?"

Happy to explain, the donut replied, "The river you arrived in comes to us from the worlds above and is constantly charging my energy. My donut-shaped body happens to be the first place where the energy is stepped down on the Alaya Lok."

"Here at the border of the seventh and eighth planes, it's my job to disperse a tiny percentage of the river's energy to the world around me. There are a total of seven donut-like cities on the seventh plane. On the sixth plane there are six. On the fifth plane you will find five. When this river finally finishes its long journey it unites with the enormous sea at the bottom of the fifth plane."

Astonished, the Caraka asked, "How many rivers are there flowing down from the higher worlds? And do any of them go all the way to the physical plane?"

The donut's bluish white light continued to sparkle as it answered, "There are countless numbers of rivers flowing down from the Ocean of Love and Joy on the Anami Lok. All these precious carriers of the Light and Sound nourish the many seas and oceans of the higher planes on a continuous basis.

"As far as I know, none of them go all the way to the physical plane. At the lower border of the fifth plane there are four massive oceans. From these large reservoirs, lower plane rivers transport their energy the rest of the way."

Appreciating what he was learning, the Caraka looked directly through the clear center of his new acquaintance and asked, "How about donut-shaped cities like you? Are there any on the lower planes?"

Realizing that the Caraka asked many questions, the donut replied, "Of course. There are donut shaped cities there as well. How else could the energy of God be dispersed? There are four on the mental plane, three on the causal plane, two on the astral plane, and one on the physical plane."

Suddenly remembering that another plane was being prepared below the physical plane, the Caraka asked curiously, "What's going to happen when the world below the physical plane is activated? Will it get a donut city, too?"

His new acquaintance quickly replied, "When events such as this occur, the planes and their accompanying donut cities are re-arranged. This may be hard for your limited level of consciousness to assimilate, but nearly a third of each plane will be pulled up into the world above it.

"This means that the highest levels of the fourth plane will receive an increase of energy and be integrated into the fifth plane. While the highest areas of the physical plane will become part of the astral plane.

"The dark world that is about to be activated below yours will merge with the bottom of the physical plane. When this happens it will receive energy from the donut city allocated to the new physical universe."

Quickly considering this vital information, the Caraka realized he had learned something of great importance. Sensing he should stop asking questions while he could still understand everything, he continued to stare through the center of his giant bluish white host for a few moments. Then he knew his class had come to an end.

Greatly appreciating what this giant donut-shaped being had shared with him, the Caraka smiled at his new friend. Then he placed his attention on his favorite chair in his room. After transporting himself there, he opened his eyes and shook his head in disbelief.

With every inner-world journey to the Alaya Lok, he was learning something way beyond him. Hopefully one day he would be able to put all the pieces of this big puzzle together.

In the meantime, the only thing he could think of was the enormous donut being and the way it altered the energy of God as it slowly descended to the lower planes.

Eventually, lower world planes and the donut cities assigned to them will be relocated to facilitate the eternal dream of our Grand Creator.

20

Learning about
the Oceans of God

The Caraka wearily sat down in his favorite chair. He had just finished a long hike in a nearby forest and needed to rest. As his energy slowly returned, he was suddenly inspired to return to the seventh plane for his next class. This was not the usual hour he did his spiritual exercises. He wondered what was compelling him to return there just now.

He closed his eyes and focused on the Master's basketball-shaped room. Milliseconds later, he spotted his mentor waiting for him. "Hello Master," he announced. "I got a sudden urge to come here for my next class! Do you have something special planned for me?"

Pleased that the Caraka had received his inter-plane call, the Master replied, "I'm going to show you something extraordinary. Are you ready?"

Curious as to what the Master considered extraordinary, the Caraka replied, "Okay, I'm ready. Let's go!"

An instant later, he felt himself being launched out the basketball-shaped room. As he flew over the giant towers of the egg-shaped city, he watched passively while the Master guided him into the ethers of the Alaya Lok.

Before too long he found himself approaching an enormous mountain—a mountain so large he estimated a fifth of the physical plane could easily fit into it.

Mindful that he was being guided to an extraordinary site, the Caraka continued to watch as he landed on the nearest flank of this massive mountain. Off in the distance he spied another egg-shaped city just like the one the Master lived in. It too had thousands of skyscraper towers surrounding an immense plaza with a round donut in its center.

This donut, however, did not have a river flowing through it. Instead, there were billions upon billions of round Soul-type beings passing through its circular core. As he continued to observe them arriving from every direction, he estimated that each being was at least fifty feet in diameter.

Once through the donut's round center, the orbs landed in a large ocean at the base of the mountain—an ocean many times larger than the mountain. Astonished that he hadn't seen it upon arrival, the Caraka wondered if he was still on the seventh plane.

Anxious to learn more about the ocean, the Caraka called out, "Dear Master, this mountain and the ocean below it appear to be so enormous that they might be larger than the entire physical plane. Is this true?"

Pleased with the Caraka's accurate assessment, the Master of the Alaya Lok replied, "Yes, they *are* larger than the physical plane. And the medium-sized Souls joining the ocean's immense body are limitless in number.

"These orbs are among the best of God's spiritual missionaries. Their sole function is to give love to the world around them. Their energy assures that the Alaya Lok functions as it does. If, for some reason, these Souls stopped emitting their love, our world could not complete its mission."

Impressed, the Caraka continued staring at the giant ocean below him in awe.

Then he asked, "Oh Master, there seem to be a lot of oceans in the worlds of God, and each one consist of countless beings emitting their love to keep everything functioning as it should. Why is this?"

Amused, the Master replied, "Oceans, my young student, are the exact replica of our Almighty Creator. Oceans nurture us and keep us alive. They also serve as storage areas where the energy of God is allowed to interact upon itself."

Sensing he was getting in over his head more quickly than usual, the Caraka gazed at the giant body before him with great admiration. Then he couldn't help but ask, "Why is God constantly creating oceans all over the place? Why doesn't it create just one big ocean and leave it at that?"

Finding the Caraka's question humorous, the Master of the Alaya Lok glimmered brightly as it replied, "That's an easy question to answer. God creates oceans in every one of its worlds because it wants its energy to continue growing."

"Before the last cycle of expansion, vast areas of complete darkness predominated. They were so dark that nothing could exist in their void. With a great need to augment the Light and Sound in these worlds, our Grand Creator began sending its little children to these areas to become creators as well."

"A similar event took place on your blue planet recently. After the last planetary shift, there were very few humans left on its surface. But, little by little humans began reproducing in order to repopulate your world. As they slowly grew in number, they became co-creators.

"Most created homes to shelter their fragile bodies, while others created farming methods which allowed them to feed themselves. This creativity was how the inhabitants of your planet used their divine energy to survive. I am pleased to say they are still creating to this day.

"The oceans of God are collecting points of energy, which permit this process to take place. They nourish your planet, making sure our Almighty Creator's plan continues. However, there are other oceans of energy surrounding your world as well. Of these vital beings humans know very little."

Finding it difficult to assimilate what the Master was sharing with him, the Caraka stopped asking questions. Instead he stared out at the giant ocean before him. As he did, he slowly mulled over the information he had just received.

From what he understood, oceans are instrumental sources of energy which enable life to grow. And God is slowly creating more and more of them in order to help his eternal children become co-Creators with It.

Feeling he had probably learned enough for one inner-world journey, the Caraka smiled brightly and thanked his giant host for guiding him there. Then he focused on his favorite chair.

The moment he arrived home, he opened his eyes and spied the yellow sun that warmed his blue planet through the open window. Finding it unusually beautiful this day, he suddenly recalled that this giant orb was covered by an enormous ocean.

This fiery ocean's loving energy radiated to the planets of his solar system in order to nourish the various life forms existing on them. Suddenly fully cognizant that the sun's giant ocean was sending its love in every direction to fulfill its vital mission, the Caraka nodded his head in appreciation.

Then he called out, "Thank you beautiful sun. Thank you for doing your part as the eternal dream of our Almighty Creator slowly materializes in the darkness of our beautiful Milky Way Galaxy.

Unseen oceans nourish planet Earth, making certain that our Almighty Creator's plans come to fruition.

21

Giving for the Good of the Whole

Mindful that he had only a few classes left on the Alaya Lok, the Caraka closed his eyes and instantly projected himself into the Master's basketball-shaped room. The moment he arrived he spied his new mentor sitting near one of the panoramic windows.

Delighted to have the opportunity to study with this grand being, the Caraka called out, "Hello Master! Thank you for the incredible classes. The seventh plane is more amazing than I ever imagined."

Aware the Caraka still had much to learn, the Master of the Alaya Lok glimmered brightly as it replied, "Yes, this world is magical. But what you've experienced here could have easily taken place on any of the planes of our Grand Creator.

"Everywhere the Ancient One sends you to study, you will find dedicated beings of the Light and Sound slowly manifesting the dream of their loving Maker. During one of your first classes, I asked you a simple question which at the time you were unable to answer. Can you answer it for me now?"

He'd completely forgotten that he had never answered the Master's question. The Caraka gleefully replied, "Yes, I do. My heart is open—at least open enough for me to travel here. But if I want to go higher, I will have to open myself up even more."

The Master's yellow light glimmered even brighter as it quickly added, "Yes, little one. Your heart is open. And I hope it stays open as you go through the difficult tests that await you on the physical plane.

"It is never easy to rejoin the river of love returning to your eternal home from the lower worlds. But if you continue to place your attention on the Light and Sound of your Divine Creator, it will be impossible to stop you. For today's class, I want to guide you to yet another important site. A site so amazing that I have left it for last. Please relax and let my energy steer you."

The Master's large body began to expand. Once it had completely surrounded him with its loving energy, the Caraka felt the Master's love massaging every atom of his tiny body.

Then a brilliant flash of yellow light picked him up as it exploded in an outward direction. Milliseconds later, the Caraka began moving at a tremendous rate of speed.

As he approached what looked to be a giant ancestor of the Milky Way Galaxy, the Caraka intuitively knew this was the site the Master had mentioned. Spinning at tremendous speed, this yellowish-white spiral was so much larger than the Milky Way that he had no way of estimating its size.

When he was almost upon it, the Master called out, "Yes, this giant helix resembles your galaxy, but I can assure you that it is much, much more. It will probably be hard for you to completely understand what I am about to tell you, but I will do my best to keep it simple.

"This spiral is at least a trillion times larger than your Milky Way Galaxy. The energy it emits is unmatched by anything you will find in the lower worlds. It has ten gigantic arms, each one set aside for the various beings of the Light and Sound existing within its loving embrace.

"You will find giant round orbs populating one arm, enormous pyramid beings coming together to form another. Smaller Milky Way clusters combine to create a third. In total there are ten different life forms united there, and their energies are perfectly balanced in order to create the extraordinary vortex of love the Alaya Lok requires for its existence.

"Eons ago, these ten teams were assigned here. The instant they arrived, they bonded effortlessly in this manner. Spinning round and round at fantastic rates, the arms emit the essential energy needed to keep the Alaya Lok going—at the same time participating in our Almighty Creator's dream.

"Since you have had a difficult time understanding basic higher world formations such as this in the past, I'll try to simplify my explanation even further. These giant arms consist of smaller beings giving of themselves so that larger life-forms can exist.

"Eons of Earth time have gone by, and these loving beings are still here, spinning round and round for the good of the whole. I know you've experienced the joy one receives when giving to others. But you have no idea what it is like to give as these being do.

"This is why I arranged for you to join them. I want you to project yourself into the central core of this ten armed Milky Way Giant in order to experience their love."

Trusting he wouldn't be knocked completely out of balance, the Caraka did his best to remain calm. Then he gently launched himself into Milky Way's inner core. An instant later, he found himself closing in on a Stonehenge-type formation made up of ten enormous obelisks rising straight up into the heavens.

The Caraka knew he had to allow the Master to finish guiding him into the center of their immense circle. As he watched passively, he glided effortlessly into the middle of these white beings. When he finally came to a stop, he saw that he was in the center of an enormous circular plaza.

As he slowly studied the impressive site, the collective telepathic voices of the ten arms called out to him, "Welcome young Caraka. We understand your concern for the energy we emit. But it has been altered to permit you access to our heart. Rest assured that you will not be destroyed or knocked out of balance.

"It's been quite a while since a traveler from the surface of planet Earth last visited us. We take this as a good sign. Close to seventy thousand years ago, Earthlings from your blue world came here on a regular basis. But this is no longer the case."

"On the behalf of your mentor, the Ancient One, you've been permitted to visit a number of sites of the Alaya Lok. As you now know it is a magical world where giving for the good of the whole is paramount for anyone wanting to partake in its consciousness. In order to familiarize yourself with the energy involved in our giving, we recommend that you relax. Then we will share with you a tiny parcel of our love."

With no idea what to expect, the Caraka courageously stared at the enormous obelisks surrounding him. Then he spied ten yellowish-white streams of light heading his way.

Each stream was flowing from the lower portion of an obelisk, and the moment they all merged with his tiny inner core, he felt a massive surge of joy penetrate his heart. This energy was like an elixir that made him happier than he had felt in a long time.

Appreciating every atom of this beautiful energy, he remained perfectly still. Then the collective voice continued, "We obelisks participate in the creation of this world. We wish you well, little one. Learn as much as you can during your spiritual journeys, and do your best to help others realize what awaits them in the inner worlds of our Almighty Creator.

"As you complete this portion of your spiritual training, the gloom and despair you have been carrying around with you will gradually disappear. It will be replaced with the feelings of joy and happiness—sensations that automatically appear when one is giving for the good of the whole.

"Now we recommend that you return to your beautiful, blue world. Return to your home and do your best to tell others about what you have learned on the Alaya Lok. As you do, you will slowly complete the mission you were assigned before your physical birth."

Amazed to have been guided to these extraordinary beings, the Caraka gazed at the ten giant obelisks surrounding him one last time. Then, he placed his attention on his quiet room on the physical plane.

The moment he opened his eyes, he looked down at the floor and shook his head in disbelief. Somehow, he was expected to re-introduce these magical sites of the higher worlds to the seekers of the Light and Sound of planet Earth. Magical sites he hardly knew anything about.

Wondering how this was going to happen, he stood up from his chair and headed for the door to take a well-deserved walk. Hoping his Master, the Ancient One, would show up during this walk to enlighten him as to how all of this was going to happen, he took a deep breath and kept walking.

Giving for the good of the whole, allows spiritual seekers to continue their journeys higher into the worlds of God.

THE TEN LORDS
OF THE HENGE

❖

22

Meeting the First Lord

A little saddened that this was his last class with the Master of the Alaya Lok, the Caraka sat down in his favorite chair. His journeys to this world had been extraordinary, and he knew he would return on his own whenever he got a chance.

Grateful he had that option, he closed his eyes. He then placed his attention on the Master's energy. An instant later, he spied his teacher on a large patio located atop the immense tower where it lived.

The building's patio afforded a panoramic view of the gigantic egg-shaped city, reminding the Caraka how large it really was. As he landed a few feet away, he wondered why his mentor was there. He looked up at the Master, who was looking off into the distance.

A few Earth seconds later, his teacher said, "Your classes on the Alaya Lok are over. You have done well and have earned the right to move on."

Feeling a sense of accomplishment, a broad smile crossed the Caraka's face. Then he watched the Master's energy begin to change. All at once, the patio floor he was standing on began slowly melting away, and he found himself flying through a portal of brilliant white light.

As his inner-world class continued, the Caraka noticed that the portal's white energy was gradually dissipating. As it disappeared completely, he found himself traveling through a tunnel of clear light.

Remembering that clear energy usually vibrates at a very high rate, he wondered if he would be able adapt to it. Suddenly, his tiny body was ejected out of the inter-plane corridor and he began looking around.

In an area of crystal clear energy, with nothing visual to guide himself by, the Caraka decided to use a technique he had learned on the Anami Lok. He placed his attention on his inner hearing. Almost instantly he heard the shrill sound of a police whistle. Sensing he must be on the right track, he continued to concentrate on this piercing sound.

Earth seconds later, he was delighted to hear a gentle telepathic voice call out to him, "Welcome young traveler from the physical plane. Your Master, the Ancient One, has arranged for you to continue your studies with me and my friends.

"You are now on the twelfth plane. The classes you are about to take here will not be as difficult as you might think. Since you recently relearned how to fine tune your inner hearing on the Anami Lok, it should be fairly simple for you to communicate with us here.

"However, I must emphasize that this plane is quite different from the Anami Lok. The Anami Lok is populated with many different groups—each dedicated to giving and receiving love. Here there are only ten beings and their assistants—each with a specific purpose.

"No one among us is considered a Master, but rather a Lord. We make up the core of the total being called the Ocean of Love and Joy. With your limited level of consciousness it will be impossible for you to completely grasp what we do. Nevertheless, we must honor the Ancient One's decision to have you study with us.

"In size, each of us is trillions upon trillions of times bigger than your physical plane. To get better acquainted with our world, I request that you shed the apprehension you are carrying with you. Do your best to relax and listen to the melodies of the other Lords surrounding me.

"We are arranged in a circular formation, similar to the ten obelisks you encountered on the Alaya Lok. But there is one enormous difference. We do not consist of the Light. Instead we are of the Sound of God. Concentrate, little one, and listen to our celestial music."

Hoping he could achieve this goal, the Caraka did his best to relax. Then he went up and down his inner hearing to locate the sounds this Lord was referring to. Soon he connected with the right frequency and clearly heard the heavenly music the Lords were emitting.

They were singing in perfect harmony. Their music was unlike any he had ever heard before. Finding it hard to distinguish their individual sounds, he listened more closely. Soon he clearly heard the precious sounds each was contributing.

He could make out an enormous bass drum beating slowly, powerful whale calls, piercing eagle chirps, wind chime notes, and trumpets blaring, as well as a number of other unexpected sounds.

They all merged together to form a perfectly balanced celestial orchestra. On and on the powerful Lords sang to the worlds they were creating, and the Caraka felt privileged to have been guided to their amazing site.

The instant he came to this realization, the soft telepathic voice continued, "I am the first Lord and when you return for your next class, you will instantly merge with the energy my assistants and I emit.

"Each class after that, you will be guided to a different Lord to enhance your knowledge of the twelfth plane. Once your studies with the ten of us come to an end, you will return to your Master, the Ancient One."

Staggered to hear what lay ahead for him, the Caraka nervously stammered, "Buuuuut, do you think I'm capable of doing this? After all, I'm pushing myself to the limit every time I travel this high. After each visit to these worlds, I return to my home feeling as if I don't belong there anymore."

The Lord remained silent as it considered his new student's concern. Then it replied, "Returning to our site will force you to reevaluate your world and possibly make you want to leave it. Nevertheless, I must remind you that you are a spiritual traveler and have been voyaging like this for more than thirty million years.

"With your current Milky Way consciousness, it might be difficult for you to grasp what I am about to tell you, but it is quite natural for you to do both. As you return to study with us, you will better understand your true function and capabilities in the worlds of the Light and Sound.

Recognizing that this super-advanced being knew more about himself than he did, the Caraka acknowledged that he could only do one thing—his best.

Delighted with the Caraka's assessment, the Lord's soft telepathic voice added, "We know you will do your best. That is the reason you will neither disappoint the Masters you work with nor yourself.

"Now it is time for you to return to your home. Go back to your beautiful blue planet, little one. As soon as you feel ready, return to this site to begin your classes. I will be waiting for you."

Eager to leave this incredible world behind, the Caraka placed his attention on his favorite chair in his room and projected himself there. The moment he opened his eyes, he shook his head in disbelief.

His recent inner-world experiences were drastically altering his level of consciousness. He hoped he could still fit into the ever-demanding society he lived in. However, apparently eons before, his eternal essence, or Soul, had entered a physical body, he had agreed to work with the Masters of the Light and Sound.

At this point, it would be spiritual suicide to change his mind, no matter how he felt or what obstacles he faced on planet Earth.

Every Soul in the lower worlds eventually gets the opportunity to study with the Ten Lords of the Ocean of Love and Joy.

23

The First Lord and the Love of Existence

Nervous about his upcoming classes with the Lords of the Twelfth Plane, the Caraka sat down on his bed. Studying with these amazing beings was not going to be easy. Questioning whether he was indeed capable of traveling to this world without being knocked out of balance, he took a few deep breaths to relax. Then he closed his eyes.

Looking at the next eleven classes as great spiritual gifts, he smiled to himself in anticipation. Then he projected himself to what the first Lord had referred to as the Ocean of Love and Joy.

Milliseconds later, he calmly scanned the clear site before him. As he did, memories of his last class returned. The twelfth plane looked exactly the same as it had during his last inner-world journey, making him aware of how limited he was there.

Certain the Lord who had welcomed him was nearby, the Caraka slowly tuned in to his inner hearing. Once more he clearly heard the shrill sound of a police whistle as it penetrated his inner core.

On Earth, the piercing blast of a police whistle usually comes to a quick end after a few bursts. But on this pristine plane it continued on and on. Surprised to find that it wasn't painful, the

Caraka decided to change the frequency of his inner hearing to locate his first mentor.

Before he could, the soft telepathic voice of the First Lord called out to him, "Welcome little one. Welcome to my world. I am looking forward to guiding you on our plane. As you can hear, the sound my donut-shaped assistants and I share with the worlds below us is similar to what you call a police whistle.

"Our melody blends in perfectly with the energy emitted by my fellow Lords and is considered the energy of love in its most primordial form. It is also known as the love of existence. Without it, you would find it impossible to survive the rigorous challenges of your world.

"Deep inside your inner core exists a great desire to survive, and this desire is connected to the sound my eternal essence creates. My love makes you want to endure the world around you. In order to better understand the importance of my energy, I have arranged for you to visit a special site. Please remain calm while I transport you there."

Hoping he was ready for the experience this amazing being was about to give him, the Caraka waited patiently. An instant later, the clear energy around him began to vibrate at a higher rate. Sensing it wise to adjust as quickly as possible, he quickly altered his inner hearing.

The equivalent of three Earth seconds later, he was surprised to hear the continuous clucking sounds of thousands of hens. On and on this strange noise continued. As it did, the Caraka suddenly lost the desire to live. Out of nowhere, he began to feel that nothing mattered. The only thing he wanted to do was sleep and disappear.

Distressed, the Caraka cried out, "I have no desire to live. Why is this so?"

Pleased to find that the Earthling was a quick learner, the First Lord calmly replied, "You have no desire to live because I guided you to an area of the ninth plane that has the power to negate my energy.

"These clucking hens, as you call them, create a sound capable of countering the will to live. Their sound is routinely employed to test advanced beings from the physical and astral planes who think they have mastered everything there is to learn about the spiritual worlds. When they are subjected to this sound, they quickly lose the will to continue their spiritual journey home. They often consider committing suicide."

This feeling had invaded him a number of times recently. The Caraka said, "This has happened to me. But my spiritual training has always helped me block out such negative thoughts. What happens to beings that have not had the opportunity to study with the Masters of the Light and Sound?"

The First Lord joyfully replied, "The clucking hen energy is extremely powerful, and when it is fully activated, even *your* spiritual training would not be sufficient to save you. Over thirty thousand years ago, your ego was so out of balance that you thought you were invincible. When you were surrounded by the energy of the clucking hens, you quickly failed this primordial test.

"The lack of the police whistle sound I emit helps spiritual students understand what it's like to turn their backs on their Grand Creator. Fortunately, the love of God never gives up on any of its creations. And in turn, It expects all of its tiny beings to never give up on It. Eventually everyone faces this test. Thus they learn how terrible it is to be blocked from the amazing energy that created them."

Relieved to know that he had taken this test a long time ago, the Caraka said, "I'm glad to know that I've faced this test before. However, recently I feel really bad at times. When I do, I want to leave my physical body behind for good. Why is this so?"

With great compassion, the First Lord replied, "Without your being aware, there is another sound that is constantly calling out to guide you home. This love of reuniting with your Eternal Maker is emitted by another Lord and I will allow that Lord to address this subject in an upcoming class."

Astonished by what he was learning, the Caraka continued to listen to the soft sound of clucking hens. He'd no idea that this noise carried with it a spiritual test. The call to destroy oneself often comes in very strongly during insurmountable situations, and one has to be careful to manage it just like any other test.

Delighted to be in the presence of the Lord who managed the energy of existence, the Caraka decided to ask one last question, "On my planet, dolphins and whales often beach themselves. Why is it that some species commit suicide en masse?"

The First Lord was silent for the equivalent of two Earth seconds. Then it replied, "Those advanced beings beach themselves for the same reason that a human takes its life.

"The surface inhabitants of your blue planet have no idea how difficult it is to survive in the life-filled oceans of your world. Fierce battles take place there every day, and the whales and dolphins often tire of this barbaric routine.

"When they commit suicide en masse, you can be certain they are being pushed to their limits. Such events could be considered wake-up calls to humans. They're a reminder of what is happening on your blue world—below the waves as well as above them."

Signaling that the Caraka's first class had come to an end, the First Lord joyfully added, "The Love of existence keeps all of God's creatures going. But in many places there is so little love that many make the decision to leave."

An instant later the soft clucking sound faded away, and the Caraka realized that the First Lord was no longer there. With his first class completed, he placed his attention on his room on planet Earth and instantly projected himself there.

He opened his eyes and absent-mindedly gazed at his feet. His encounter with the First Lord of the Twelfth Plane had gone well, and he had come to an interesting conclusion.

No matter how bad things appeared to be on his blue planet, the Love of Existence was there to guide him. Knowing this comforted him greatly.

Whenever an old Soul thinks It's invincible, the energy of the Clucking Hens descends from the ninth plane to test It.

24

The Second Lord
and the Love of Life

Closing his eyes, the Caraka took a few deep breaths. His recent inner-world journey with the First Lord had surprised him greatly, and he couldn't help wondering what awaited him next. Hoping his next class would be just as easy, he projected himself into the circular formation where the Lords awaited him.

Earth-seconds later, he recalibrated his inner hearing. It was eerily silent and he questioned if he had returned to the right place. It appeared as if he was all alone. Not sure it was wise for him to explore this world on his own, he came to a complete stop. A powerful energy slowly wrapped itself around his tiny body.

Wondering what was happening to him, he concentrated fully on his inner hearing and instantly heard the celestial music of the Lord closest to him.

Its energy was quite soft, and as the Caraka listened closely he clearly heard its soft telepathic voice whisper, "Welcome little one. I am the Second Lord of the Twelfth Plane. I will be your mentor for this class. To begin, I would like you to concentrate on my eternal melody."

Eager to comply, the Caraka focused intently on this being's energy. Instantly he was overpowered by the intense incantations of an enormous whale. This celestial chanting was slightly lower in pitch than the sound emitted by the First Lord, but its intensity seemed to be just as powerful.

Wondering what he was, in fact, listening to, the Caraka concentrated even harder. Right away, he discovered that the energy of the Second Lord was carrying him away. Traveling on the waves of this powerful whale music, he listened more intently until he realized that he was approaching yet another Stonehenge-type structure.

This structure was located inside a giant transparent cloud, and when he was almost upon it, he recognized that it was much different from the first one. Instead of ten giant, clear, obelisks, there appeared to be hundreds of smaller ones arranged in an enormous circle.

Wondering why he had been brought here, the Caraka calmly asked, "Second Lord, did you guide me to this site for my next class?"

Pleased, the Lord joyfully replied, "You are in the middle of my small henge. From here my eternal energy is transmitted to the worlds below us. The small singing obelisks are my assistants, and we love each other dearly.

"Our music is known as the Love of Life. It permits every being of God to love himself as a combination of living energies. Every tree, human, insect, ocean, mountain, planet, microbe, sun, solar system, and universe needs my energy. Without it, they would slowly collapse in on themselves."

Pleased to be able to understand this, the Caraka asked, "Does this energy come standard for everyone, or do you have to change the voltage for each life form you send it to? For example, does a rabbit get the same type of energy as our yellow sun gets?"

There was a short pause. Then the Second Lord of the Twelfth Plane continued, "A rabbit on your planet does not receive the same type of energy as your sun does. It is given energy that is processed through two additional sites that are modeled after this henge.

"Most of the mammals of your planet fall into the same category, while the insects of your world receive energy that is processed yet an additional time. You humans fit into two groups. The less advanced receive the same energy as many of the evolved animals. Earthlings with higher levels of consciousness receive energy that has been processed one less time.

"Mountains, deserts, lakes and rivers of the physical plane also fall into this category. Humans capable of qualifying for this higher group are more celestial by nature. They have been trained lifetime after lifetime to handle the power of higher energy. Suns and stars, meanwhile, fall into a category three levels higher."

Amazed, the Caraka looked at the hundreds of transformer-like beings surrounding him. Then he asked, "Your assistants must be receiving energy that is much more powerful than our sun. Can you give me an estimate as to how powerful this energy is?"

Pleased with the Caraka's many questions, the Second Lord's soft telepathic voice replied, "The sound they process is at least twenty thousand times stronger than the energy your yellow sun receives. Energy this powerful is not found anywhere near the lower worlds. In fact, what is emitted here never drops below the ninth plane. If it did, it would create havoc with the life forms living below us."

Wondering why this powerful energy hadn't yet annihilated him, the Caraka had to ask, "How is it I'm able to travel here? Did I receive special training eons ago that I know nothing about?"

Finding the Caraka's question amusing, the Second Lord seemed to chuckle as it answered, "Your tiny essence is originally from this plane. For this reason, you fit right in. However, if you had been able to travel here in your physical body, it would have disintegrated the moment you arrived."

Appreciating that the Lord seemed to enjoy answering his questions, the Caraka asked another, "When I first arrived, you informed me that your energy is considered the Love of Life. Does this mean that the whale sounds you emit travel throughout the worlds of God to make everyone and everything love their lives?"

Remaining silent for a few Earth seconds, the Second Lord replied, "For the most part, I have to say this is true. However, in a few select areas, my whale sounds must pass through special transformers to alter the intensity of my energy.

"These special sites are nothing like the worlds humans are assigned to. Mountains, rivers, stars, and galaxies do not exist there. Nor do any of the beings that inhabit the planes your Masters have guided you to so far.

"Because of this difference, you would be at a complete loss how to exist in these worlds. As far as I know, no orb of your stature has ever been allowed to visit one of these magical sites."

His curiosity piqued, the Caraka queried, "Where are these special worlds located? And what kinds of beings live there?"

The Second Lord replied succinctly, "There are two of these special worlds on the seventh plane. They are populated by beings that are nebulous in nature. They can best be described as gigantic energy fields."

Intrigued, the Caraka asked, "If I'm not mistaken, you Lords of the Twelfth Plane are gigantic energy fields. How is it that I can communicate with you, but not with the ones on the seventh plane?"

Enjoying their conversation, the Lord replied, "In essence we are enormous energy fields. But what makes us different from the beings on the seventh plane is that we generate more love. And our love is directly linked to the little spark of energy that makes up your inner core.

"The beings of the seventh plane generate much less love. For this reason, it would be impossible for you to participate in their worlds. Their levels of consciousness are so different from what you are accustomed to, that it would be impossible for you to understand anything they do."

Sensing there was no point in asking additional questions about these beings, the Caraka stared silently at the circle of obelisks surrounding him.

Then, feeling privileged to have communicated with this amazing being, the Caraka said, "Thank you, Second Lord, for explaining what you do in such a simple manner. During my upcoming classes I aspire to learn more about the other members of your group and what you do here."

Certain his second class with this great being had come to an end, the Caraka listened closely to the soft loving whale music of his mentor and its assistants. Then he placed his attention on his room on the physical plane.

The moment he arrived, he opened his eyes and looked out the window across the room. Seeing the brilliant yellow sun that warms his planet in the distance, he felt a surge of love grow in his heart.

He had just learned that this yellow sun receives energy different from his. Nevertheless, this difference didn't stop them from communicating with each other.

Gratefully, the Caraka cried out, "Thank you, beautiful sun, for doing your part in keeping us all alive. Without your version of the Love of Life, it would be impossible for anything to exist on our precious, but challenging, blue planet.

Celestial Whale Music created by the Second Lord,
carries with it the eternal Love of Life.

25

The Third Lord and the Eternal Beat of Love

Plopping down in his favorite chair, the Caraka gazed out the window of his room. It was a sunny Saturday morning and he intuitively felt this was the perfect time to do his spiritual exercise.

Expecting to learn something amazing, he closed his eyes and projected himself to the clear world of the twelfth plane. When he arrived, he placed his attention on his inner hearing and was surprised to hear the soft sound of a giant bass drum beating at regular intervals. Its long drawn-out notes were super-soft. So soft that they blended in perfectly with the world surrounding him.

As he listened, he was pleased to hear a gentle voice call out to him, "Welcome back young Caraka. I am the Third Lord of the Twelfth Plane and will be your guide for this inner-world journey. The beats you hear are not being emitted by a giant drum, but by my assistants and I. Because they help me complete my mission, I feel it is important that you meet them."

Almost instantly, the energy of the site began to change. Assuming the Third Lord was transporting him to its own area of the twelfth plane, the Caraka watched with great anticipation. When he finally came to a stop, he found that he had been guided to another site of clear energy, similar to the other clear areas of this world he had visited up till now—with one exception.

The vibrations were so powerful that it felt as if he was standing in the middle of an enormous drum. On and on, the slow rhythmic notes of the site continued. The Caraka wondered if these powerful beats would overwhelm him.

Wanting to avoid this, the Caraka cried out, "Oh Lord, your-drum beats are very, very powerful. I doubt I can stay here very long. Can you please tell me the purpose they serve and who produces them?"

Conscious of the Caraka's concern, the Third Lord joyfully replied, "The beings emitting my celestial sound could be considered highly-calibrated crystals. They are precise to the tiniest fraction. They have been in charge of emitting the pulse of God since the beginning of creation. It is the eternal cadence that guides all the worlds of our Almighty Creator. And every being below this plane is synchronized to it."

Astonished to learn that the Universes of God were all working off the same beat, the Caraka asked, "Does this mean that even a worm living in the ground on my planet is tuned in to this pulse and that it depends on it for guidance?"

The soft voice of the Third Lord continued, "Yes, little one. That little creature is in complete harmony with my energy. All of its actions, whether obvious or not, are synchronized with me and my crystalline assistants."

Confused, the Caraka remained silent, listening to the intense pounding. Finally he just had to ask, "What would happen if these crystal-like beings were to skip a beat or change somehow? Would everything continue the same? Or would there be problems throughout the planes below us."

Wanting to explain these eternal beats in a manner the Caraka could understand, the Lord said, "Let's pretend you are driving down the highway in your car at sixty miles per hour. As you're cruising along, the timing of your motor suddenly changes. What would happen?"

Pleased to have an answer, the Caraka replied, "Well, if you're fortunate, your motor would simply shut down and you would come to a complete stop. If you're not fortunate, your motor would seize up, causing major damage, possibly destroying the crankshaft, pistons and casing."

Delighted with his student's answer, the Third Lord continued, "That's right. There are all sorts of consequences when one does something as simple as changing the timing of a motor. The same thing would happen if you changed the timing of the worlds of God.

"All the planets, rivers, mountains, and other bodies of God that you are completely unaware of, would either seize up or launch themselves in directions they were never intended to go."

Finally aware of how important these giant crystals were, the Caraka listened intently to their perfect cadence. Their precise love still felt overwhelming to him, but it didn't seem to affect him as much as it had in the beginning.

He had somehow become accustomed to the steady rhythm and was certain he could remain there now. Relieved, the Caraka remained silent as the powerful drum beats continued passing through him.

Then he gratefully called out, "Third Lord, I want to thank you for introducing me to your amazing crystal assistants. I had no idea that our Almighty Creator emits an eternal beat of love that keeps everything running smoothly. Thank you!"

Ready to return to his blue world, the Caraka placed his attention on his quiet room on planet Earth. The moment he felt the cushion of his chair underneath him, he opened his eyes and placed his attention on his internal hearing one last time.

There it was. The thump, thump, thump of the giant bass drum he had just left behind on the twelfth plane. It was still with him. Faint, but it was there nevertheless. Now that he knew who created it and where it came from, he would listen for it more often to synchronize himself with its eternal love.

*Without the synchronized pulse of the love of
the Third Lord, the worlds of God would
instantly seize up and cease to exist.*

26

The Fourth Lord and the Love of Creation

Amazed by what he was learning on the Twelfth Plane, the Caraka strolled over to his favorite chair and sat down. The moment he was comfortable, he closed his eyes and focused in on the site of the Ten Lords. Almost instantly, he found himself in the middle of their sacred energy.

Delighted to be starting his next class, he slowly perused his inner hearing. The first sound he tuned in to reminded him of countless trumpets calling out to the world around them.

Feeling the intense power they were wielding, he knew it would be impossible for him to stay there very long. Wanting to find out who was producing this blaring melody before he was forced to leave, he continued focusing on their powerful notes.

Three Earth seconds later, a soft telepathic voice called out to him, "Welcome young seeker from the physical plane. I am the Fourth Lord. For this class I would like to introduce you to the energy my assistants and I create.

"The trumpet sound you hear exemplifies the love that my small band and I produce. Our love is used for the creation of the almost limitless life-forms constantly being conceived in the worlds below us. Even your small physical body was created with the energy we emitted millions of years ago."

Surprised to find he existed due to beings that sounded like blaring trumpets, the Caraka asked, "Can you please explain how your energy is instrumental in forming the life-forms living in the lower worlds?"

Having anticipated the Caraka's question, the Fourth Lord replied, "I, as the Fourth Lord of the Twelfth Plane, emit a special note that has the capacity to create life. Once my note leaves me, a group of my assistants has the responsibility to guide it to another group of assistants. The third group automatically propels my love to the lower planes.

"All of us combine our expression of love to guarantee that a celestial creation, such as you, is complete. But my sacred melody, or love, is the actual energy that gets the process started."

Sensing he was missing something, the Caraka timidly asked, "Can you tell me how all of this comes together in a more explicit manner?

The Fourth Lord seemed to chuckle as it joyfully asked, "How about if I guide you through the process? This way you can experience it for yourself?"

An instant later, the Caraka felt his tiny essence propelled into the vastness of the twelfth plane. On and on he traveled, until he finally stopped in the middle of an immense void. Realizing he had to recalibrate his inner hearing to continue his class, the Caraka slowly traveled up his auditory scale.

Almost instantly, he could clearly hear trillions upon trillions of obelisks emitting a powerful sound. This sound bore a great resemblance to a sacred word he frequently chanted when he did his spiritual exercises.

Caught completely off guard, the Caraka listened closely as these powerful obelisks trumpeted the word HU to the world around them. HUUUUUUUUUUUUUUUUUUUU, HUUUUUUUUUUUUUUU, HUUUUUUUUUUUUUUUU.

Amazed to discover that this heavenly sound originated here, the Caraka wondered how it affected the worlds below them. Suddenly, the energy of the Fourth Lord picked him up for a second time. Five Earth seconds later, he found himself approaching an enormous white river on the seventh plane.

When he was the equivalent of an Earth mile away, the telepathic voice of the Fourth Lord continued, "The Love of HU, which is created by my assistants and I, flows in a downward direction until it is collected on the Anami Lok— or the tenth plane of God. There it falls in the form of tiny droplets to join the giant ocean of that world.

Once collected, it continues its journey to the lower worlds in the giant river you see before you.

"A short distance from here, our eternal essence flows into the giant ocean of the seventh plane. This process of going from river to ocean takes place on five different planes before our HU energy finally arrives on the physical plane."

He had understood everything up to this point, so the Caraka asked another question, "Where does the energy arriving on the physical plane actually come from?"

An instant later, the Caraka was projected to a third site. Once his tiny body began to slow down, he recognized that he was being guided over an enormous ocean of yellowish-orange light. Then an enormous super sun flashed before him.

The Caraka listened closely as the Fourth Lord continued, "I just steered you past the giant ocean of the causal plane that nourishes the physical and astral planes. Now you are in the presence of a newly-formed sun on the outskirts of the Milky Way.

"This sun is being nourished from the causal plane, but its initial energy was created by me and my assistants emitting HU on the twelfth plane. Once our love reaches the physical plane, it is transferred to yet another group of assistants who are in charge of creating molds for these types of life-forms.

"Eons ago, they received our HU energy and filled the mold they created to bring this sun to life. Shortly thereafter, the remaining Lords added their particular love to give it the different kinds of energy it needed.

"Their love was added in a proper sequence. Every form of life is created using this simple but efficient process—even your physical body."

Admiring the newly-created sun glowing before him, the Caraka had to mull over what the Forth Lord was telling him. Placing this sun on the physical plane seemed to be a simple enough process. However, one part continued to elude him.

With great curiosity he asked, "I think I understand just about everything. However, how does the energy from the causal plane get here to nourish this young sun?"

Having anticipated the Caraka's question, the Fourth Lord replied, "This newborn orb receives its energy through a giant portal located a short distance from here. Portals are similar to the stop lights that manage automobile traffic all over your planet. When the light is green, the energy from the causal plane arrives to feed your world. When it's red, it stops. There are billions of them in your universe and they serve the growing needs of your ever-expanding world.

"Fortunately, the scientists of your world are finally studying these magical doorways. Soon they will unlock the secret as to how this energy arrives. Until they do, you will have to take my word for it."

Amazed, the Caraka continued staring at the new sun in front of him. Then he decided he'd better place his attention on his physical body sitting patiently for him in his favorite chair.

The instant he arrived, he raised his left hand and looked into his palm. It wasn't every day that he studied the handiwork of his body, but this seemed like the perfect time.

After a short examination, he concluded that the Fourth Lord and its assistants had done an amazing job. The mold they had created with their love was perfect. And the HU energy nourishing the tiny cells of his hand was precious beyond words.

The HU, created by the Fourth Lord and its assistants, is the eternal essence that permits life to exist.

27

The Fifth Lord and the Fiery Love of God

After finishing his evening meal, the Caraka climbed the steps to his room two at a time. He was greatly enjoying his experiences on the twelfth plane. They were way beyond anything he had done up till now, but surprisingly easy.

Wondering what awaited him next, he closed the door to his room and walked over to his favorite chair. Sitting down, he closed his eyes and placed his attention on the circular site where the Ten Lords normally gathered and began to project himself there.

An instant later, he surveyed the clear energy of their world. He could easily feel the love the Lords were emitting. He concluded that it was extremely powerful—but extremely soft at the same time.

Knowing he had to fine-tune his inner hearing to continue, he concentrated on the sounds around him. Earth seconds later, he clearly heard what he could only describe as the collective call of a large herd of elephants.

Their sound was quite harmonious, and as he listened intently he realized that the elephant calls were carrying him away. Knowing he had to remain calm, the Caraka allowed the elephant voices to steer him.

The moment he stopped, he recognized that he had been guided to a site unlike any he had ever visited before. Feeling extremely intense energy passing through his tiny body, he began to fine tune his inner hearing in order to adapt.

He raised it to a slightly higher level and immediately encountered an enormous fire burning completely out of control in every direction. Somehow the beings making these elephant calls were also creating this fire. Unable to clearly make out what these beings looked like, the Caraka continued listening to their powerful elephant-like calls.

Ten Earth seconds later, a soft telepathic voice called out, "Welcome young Caraka. Welcome to the Holy Fire of your Almighty Creator. I am the Fifth Lord of the Twelfth Plane and will be your mentor during this inner-world journey."

"The love that my assistants and I produce is fiery by nature. And fire of any type corresponds to energy. The love we create is similar to something in fashion on your planet a century ago.

"When furnaces were in use, coal and wood were thrown into them to warm your homes and buildings. Although quite primitive, this system kept humans from freezing. We have the same responsibility, but on a much grander scale."

"I understand how a furnace works," the Caraka said. "However, I have no idea how your group is able to heat a galaxy or solar system of the physical plane. Can you please give me a simple explanation?"

Pleased with the Caraka's interest, the Fifth Lord replied, "In order to receive an answer to your question, you must alter your perspective of how a furnace works. The furnace of God is much larger than the little ones in use on Earth.

"God's furnace is so enormous that it includes every being ever created in the worlds below us. Every one of God's little offspring has the equivalent of a tiny furnace imbedded in its internal essence. This gives them all the capability to receive the fiery love my assistants and I emit to stay alive.

"Our special waves might sound like elephant calls to you. But they are much, much more. Without this energy, or love, your eternal essence, or Soul, would cease to exist within milliseconds.

"Once you, as Soul, perish, all the functions taking place in your physical body would come to a quick halt."

Astonished to hear that he and his body were kept alive by fiery beings that sounded like giant elephants, the Caraka continued, "I think I understand how an individual Soul, like me, receives this fiery love. But how does a giant being like a planet or sun receive it?"

Enjoying the Caraka's simple questions, the Fifth Lord replied, "It will probably surprise you to learn that your planet and everything on it receives our energy in the same way you do.

"On every plane there are millions upon millions of wheels receiving our energy. The wheels could be compared to your body's chakras. They have the capacity to reach every form of life in existence. Once our fiery love passes through one of these chakras, it is quickly absorbed and then internally dispersed through a being such as your sun.

"I have often compared sun-beings to giant multi-colored flowers receiving their nourishment from our eternal source on the twelfth plane. Once they are fed, they send their precious energy into the darkness of space to give life to others. These precious beings have been designed to pass on our love to everything that exists in their realm."

Finding it interesting that the Fifth Lord would compare his planet's sun to an enormous flower, the Caraka continued with his questions. "Since your fiery love is emitted everywhere, I should be able to see it. Can you tell me what it looks like?"

The Fifth Lord instantly replied. "Your physical eyes cannot perceive these wave lengths. It is impossible for you to see them. However, if you still your inner hearing and listen, you will be able to hear it clearly. It is constantly permeating your world and is known as the 'music of the spheres' by the few humans who have heard it."

Wondering if he was able to hear this music, the Caraka gratefully replied, "The moment I get home, I'll listen for your fiery love. Does it sound like a muted version of the giant chorus of elephants of this plane?"

Wanting the Caraka to get this right, the Fifth Lord replied, "No. Our sound is different on every plane. I recommend that you make an effort to find out for yourself what it is on the physical plane.

"Return to the comfort of your quiet room and listen for the fiery love permeating your world. I'm sure you'll be able to identify it quite easily. Remember, it is the precious essence that nourishes you."

Captivated to know he was equipped with an internal furnace capable of processing the fiery love of God, the Caraka placed his attention on his favorite chair in his room. When he arrived, he remembered to keep his eyes closed. Then he listened intently to the world around him.

Seconds later, he clearly heard the high pitched noise that follows him everywhere. It reminded him of a high pitched sound that a tea kettle produces when the water inside it begins boiling. Ever since he was a small child, he could remember doing his best to ignore it.

But as he had just learned, this fiery love of God had traveled a long way to get here to sustain life on the physical plane. Considered the equivalent of wood or coal thrown into a furnace, every human's life would instantly end without it.

Every human is equipped with a tiny furnace capable of processing the tea kettle sound of the fiery love of God.

28

The Sixth Lord and the Love of Peace

Eager to continue his classes on the twelfth plane, the Caraka sat down on his bed. Once he was comfortably seated, he closed his eyes. Then he projected himself into the area where he normally encountered the Ten Lords.

Wanting to begin as quickly as possible, he focused in on the clear energy surrounding him. Five Earth seconds later, he was pleased to hear the Ten Lords singing their celestial melodies in harmony.

Looking forward to learning something amazing, he listened intently to their loving voices. Then he felt the energy of the lord closest to him encircle his tiny body. An instant later, the Caraka watched with great curiosity as he was propelled to the outskirts of the twelfth plane.

When he finally came to a stop, he was in yet another desolate site. Unable to see a thing, he slowly adjusted his inner hearing to his surroundings.

Then he heard a soft voice call out to him, "Welcome, young Caraka. Welcome to my special site. I am the Sixth Lord of the Twelfth Plane, and I hereby invite you to join me and my assistants as we fulfill our spiritual destiny. My team and I have been living here for eons in order to participate in the eternal expansion of the worlds below us. I invite you to join us."

Sensing he once again had to fine-tune his inner hearing up a level, the Caraka made this minor adjustment. Then he clearly heard what he could only describe as trillions upon trillions of giant cats crying out to each other in perfect harmony. "Meow, meow, meow," they sang. The Caraka wondered if he was hearing correctly. A little confused, he couldn't imagine how this sound could possibly help the worlds of God grow.

Curiosity piqued, he asked, "Can you please tell me how your celestial music is participating in the eternal expansion of the worlds below us?"

Delighted that he had asked, the Sixth Lord replied, "These cat calls, as you call them, are created by enormous beings that are commonly known on your planet as star clusters. They emit a form of love that is unknown on the physical plane—a love consisting of peace. Wherever it is heard, peace reigns.

"After we create our love, it is guided to a number of the planes below us. But it goes no further than the bottom of the sixth plane. The lack of our love on the lower planes reflects the lack of peace found in these worlds. They are worlds of perpetual change and will remain so until our celestial music is allowed to flourish there."

He had never imagined there was such a thing as a love that consisted of peace. The Caraka asked, "How come I've never heard of this love before?"

The Sixth Lord promptly replied, "You have never heard of this love because it is only of value to those who use it in the higher worlds. No one in the lower worlds has any need for our energy. For this reason they know nothing about it."

Finding all of this very interesting, the Caraka asked, "I know the fifth plane is part of the higher worlds. Why doesn't this energy travel there as well?"

Anticipating the Caraka's question, the Sixth Lord answered, "The fifth plane is located on the border of the higher and lower worlds. For this reason it gets treated differently. The moment our pure love reaches the top of the fifth plane, it is converted into the positive, negative, and neutral energies required for the lower worlds. From that point on, our energy is no longer as pure as when we originally created it."

Saddened that the lower worlds aren't allowed to share in this peace-creating melody, the Caraka listened more closely to the cat-like meowing created by the Sixth Lord and its assistants. It didn't seem fair to him that the worlds of God had been arranged in this manner. But that's how it was.

Remembering that the lower planes are spiritual schools set up to teach students how to work with the love and power allocated to them in their dark worlds, the Caraka wanted to know more about his Almighty Creator and its plans for expansion.

Hoping the lower worlds could raise their levels of consciousness sometime soon in order to share in this love, he concentrated intently on the trillions of beings surrounding him.

A few Earth minutes later, he discovered that their eternal peace was penetrating deeper and deeper into his inner core. Suddenly feeling whole for the first time in ages, he wondered if this was the only way to connect with this energy of pure peace.

The Caraka called out, "Oh Sixth Lord, at least two times a day, I travel to the higher worlds. Once I arrive, I do my best to fill myself with the peace that exists on those planes. Is there a way to do this on the physical plane as well? Even if the energy of pure peace does not travel to my world?"

Recognizing the Caraka's craving for this elusive love, the Sixth Lord replied, "For hundreds of thousands of years, the Masters of the Light and Sound of your planet have been chanting sacred mantras.

"When sung with love, these special words have the ability to fill any human with the peace of the higher planes. This can be done while you are in your physical body, but the energy of love must be included. Love is the key that opens this magical door."

He had been doing exactly this for at least twenty-five years. The Caraka continued to listen to the immense cat chorus of the twelfth plane. As he absorbed their beautiful melody, he suddenly had a question completely unrelated to what they were discussing.

Hoping the Sixth Lord could answer it, the Caraka asked, "Why is it that the beings of your world chant sounds that correspond to animals of my world?"

Pleased with the Caraka's question, the Sixth Lord answered, "Animals are creatures of God just like you. Their tiny essence as Soul is connected to their eternal home and they sing the way they do because the essence of their DNA originates on the twelfth plane. They are programmed to call out to each other in the same manner that we do, using very similar sounds.

The Master continued, "Love needs to be shared in order to be enjoyed. The little animals that meow to each other on your planet are doing just that, sharing their love with one another!"

The Caraka smiled in appreciation. He was learning much more than he had anticipated about the various sounds of God. But now it was time to return to his home.

Before he did, he called out to the Sixth Lord, "Thank you for sharing your love of peace with me. This energy is very difficult to live without. Now that I know it originates here I will return to visit you often."

Full of gratitiude for everything he had learned on this inner-world journey, the Caraka placed his attention on his favorite chair. When he opened his eyes an instant later, he found himself in a daze.

Since he could do very little at the moment, he stared out the window. It was a beautiful afternoon, and as he observed the fluffy clouds floating in the blue sky he began to review what he had just learned.

It was amazing to think that the meowing sound created by the millions of cats of his planet originated on the twelfth plane. Constantly emitted by the Sixth Lord and his assistants, it expressed pure peace, a form of love that never reached the lower worlds.

Quickly considering the many four-legged, feline characters he had run into over the years, he decided his Almighty Creator had chosen wisely. These finicky mammals seemed to crave peace at all costs, doing whatever they could to avoid the constant turmoil surrounding them.

The pure energy of eternal peace currently stops at the top of the fifth plane, and will remain there until the lower worlds have earned the right to receive it.

29

The Seventh Lord and the Love That Binds Everything Together

Extremely tired, the Caraka returned to his home after a busy day at work. Certain he would have little trouble sleeping that night, he finished his evening meal and slowly climbed the steps to his room. Then he settled down into his favorite chair.

Hoping to find his next inner-world class an easy one, he closed his eyes. Then he placed his attention on the area where he always met the Lords of the Twelfth Plane. An instant later, he recalibrated his inner hearing and clearly heard the celestial melody of the Ten Lords.

As he listened closely, a soft note he had failed to identify earlier penetrated his tiny core. Wondering what it could be, he placed his attention directly on it. Two Earth minutes later, he realized it had two aspects. One was very powerful and reminded him of thunder, while the other was soft and sounded like a flute.

Finding it hard to accept that the sound of a flute could be as powerful as thunder, the Caraka continued concentrating on this soothing but formidable energy. As he did, he came to the realization that his tiny body had been surrounded by this sound. Next he found himself being guided into the ethers of the twelfth plane.

When he finally came to a stop, a soft telepathic voice called out to him, "Welcome young Caraka. I am the Seventh Lord of the Twelfth Plane, and I welcome you to my world. While guiding you here, I overheard your thoughts concerning the music my assistants and I create. I would like to share with you more about our love.

"As you just discovered, the sound we create is similar to what you call a flute. However, as we create this energy, or love, we put so much of ourselves into it that it can be compared to the loudest thunder in all of the universes of God."

Curious as to what type of beings were actually creating this music, the Caraka asked, "What do your assistants look like?"

Delighted with the Caraka's question, the Seventh Lord replied, "Each of my assistants resembles a large mass of clear energy many times larger than your physical universe.

"There are six in total, and the clear sound we emit as a group is the love needed to keep all of the worlds below us together. The strength of our energy is unequaled and could be considered the cosmic glue of God."

Having never heard of such energy before, the Caraka responded, "I don't recall hearing of a love that binds everything together. Can you please tell me more about it?"

The Seventh Lord joyfully continued, "The energy we create is quite basic and has been programmed to travel to every plane below us. To better understand how it works, I would like to take you on a short tour."

Sensing he was about to learn something extremely important, the Caraka waited patiently as the Seventh Lord's clear energy began vibrating at a higher rate. A split second later, he found himself in the middle of the henge-like site where the Lord and its mighty assistants create their powerful music.

The assistants were endless in size and as the Caraka continued listening to their powerful melody, he recognized that their eternal voices were everywhere. Suddenly he found himself being propelled through a number of regions in their vast domain.

As he flew at an incredible speed, it dawned on him that he was descending from one plane to another. Able to identify distinct worlds, he concluded two things. First, he had visited many of these sites before. Second, the flute melody produced by these enormous, clear, beings was indeed keeping everything together. Somehow, the love produced by the Seventh Lord and its enormous assistants completely surrounded all the planes below them.

Wondering if he might be missing something, the Caraka asked another question, "Are there other beings helping you produce this cosmic glue?"

The Seventh Lord immediately replied, "We are the only ones assigned with the responsibility of keeping the planes together. No one else is capable of doing what we do."

Listening to the thunderous call of the flute permeating all the worlds below the twelfth plane, the Caraka realized that their celestial call was so mighty that it made it impossible for any of God's worlds to get lost in the darkness surrounding them.

Knowing that the Caraka would soon be overwhelmed by the power of this love, the soft telepathic voice of the Seventh Lord interjected, "Little one. It is time for you to go home. Return to your small blue planet to enjoy the gifts of love that await you there.

"However, whenever you have some free time, I suggest you listen for our beautiful melody of the flute as it permeates your world. As you listen to it, remember that it originates on the twelfth plane and that its endless love keeps all of God's creations united as one."

Taken completely by surprise by this celestial glue, the Caraka placed his attention on his favorite chair in his room. The moment he opened his eyes, he shook his head in disbelief.

Since his first inner-world journey to the twelfth plane, he had been receiving information so amazing that he doubted he would ever completely understand what the Ten Lords were trying to teach him. But he had to do his best. He began to review his last class with the Seventh Lord. As he did, he heard the single note of a flute and immediately recognized it for what it was—the powerful cosmic glue of the twelfth plane.

Focusing in intently on its energy, he took it as a confirmation—a confirmation that he would eventually understand how all the love of God bonds together. Regardless of his limited human level of consciousness.

The celestial call of the flute is so mighty, that it keeps all the worlds of God below the twelfth plane united as one.

30

The Eighth Lord and the Love to Return to Our Eternal Home

Wanting a few minutes alone, the Caraka slowly closed the door to his room behind him. Some of his friends were watching a football game downstairs, and he had decided to sneak away for a while. Hoping they wouldn't come looking for him, he sat down in his favorite chair and gazed into his third eye.

Needing to complete his eighth class as quickly as possible, he projected himself to the twelfth plane of God. He then placed his attention on his inner hearing. The equivalent of four Earth seconds later, he heard what he could only describe as the vowel "E" being repeated over and over again.

This powerful sound permeated the ethers of the site where he normally met the Lords, and the Caraka could tell that this "E" energy was having a special effect on him. Wanting to learn more about it, he listened with great interest. Suddenly he was whisked away to an area of the twelfth plane he had never visited before.

Just like all the other sites of this world, it consisted completely of clear light. When the "E" energy finally released him, he had to recalibrate his inner hearing. Not wanting to miss a thing, he raised it a notch higher. Then he listened more intently as the celestial "E" call grew louder and louder.

When it began to overwhelm him, he realized that he was surrounded by millions upon millions of large, clear orbs. They were the creators of this magical sound, and he was delighted to have identified them so easily.

Listening intently, he clearly heard a soft telepathic voice call out to him, "Welcome, young traveler from the physical plane. Welcome to our world of pure love. I am the Eighth Lord, and the *EEEEEEEEE, EEEEEEEEE, EEEEEEEEE* music you hear is our celestial call. It is vital for every being ever created in the higher worlds.

"Our melody is one of the ten energies of love of the twelfth plane, and a tiny segment of it is placed in every sub-atomic molecule born here. It is essentially a higher-plane passport which permits you to return to our world whenever you will it to be so."

Delighted to have understood everything to this point, the Caraka asked, "How does a being from the physical plane will himself to return here?"

"This might come as a surprise," the Eighth Lord of the Twelfth Plane replied, "but it isn't difficult for a human to travel here from the physical plane. What is difficult is connecting with the eternal roadmap imbedded deep inside you.

"Since you've been living on a planet located on the outskirts of the physical universe, you know very little about the higher worlds. Nevertheless, intergalactic visitors have been assigned to your planet to help humans raise their limited levels of consciousness.

"Your roadmap is vital. And, like any other map, it allows you to comprehend what exists outside your world. For example, every human on Earth knows that Pluto is on the outskirts of your solar system. Why do human know this? Because they learned about it in school at an early age.

"Have they ever seen this celestial orb with their own eyes? Probably not. But this doesn't negate its existence or the fact that everyone knows it exists. Once a human accepts that the twelfth plane exists, getting here will not be that difficult. All one has to do is place his attention on it.

"Making this huge leap in consciousness will enable the spiritual beings of your planet to re-activate the roadmap of the inner worlds of God that is embedded in their tiny core, or Soul. Only then will Earthlings be free to travel wherever they wish to go."

Pleased to understand the Eighth Lord's simple explanation, the Caraka asked, "What would be the best way to help someone if they asked me how to get started?"

Delighted with the Caraka's question, the Lord joyfully replied, "The best way is to teach the importance of linking up with the eternal essence of the Almighty Creator. Once one makes this simple connection, he will access the immense love found deep inside himself.

"This precious energy permits one to activate what could be called the inner-world passport. Once activated, this passport will grant access to the worlds above the physical planes.

"Upon using it a few times, a being will easily recognize the unrelenting desire to return to its eternal home."

Surprised by the Lord's answer, the Caraka had another question. "I've lived in many places on my blue planet. But no matter where I lived, I found myself repeating over and over, "I want to go home, I want to go home." Is the love that you and your assistants emit on the twelfth plane connected with this ceaseless desire?"

Wanting the Caraka to correctly understand this important phenomenon, the Lord calmly replied, "You are not alone in repeating those words. In fact, every being of the lower worlds is seeking to return to its eternal home, just as you are.

"All of them are constantly yearning for the pure love, joy, peace, and tranquility found above the fifth plane. However, there is a third step you should know about. Once a spiritual being discovers the passport hidden inside his inner core and begins traveling with the roadmap, something else happens quite naturally.

"Every traveler makes contact with my assistants and me. This contact will hardly be perceptible at first. But once it is made, the roadmap will grow exponentially, allowing him to visit worlds he has no idea even exist.

"At first, most humans project themselves to sites close to the physical plane. But eventually they travel to temples of the Light and Sound established on each plane by the spiritual hierarchy. There they gain the needed knowledge to travel higher.

"Now little one, your class is over. Please return to your blue planet. Return to your home and do your best to help others discover the eternal passports they have hidden deep inside their tiny bodies."

Impressed with the outcome of this class, the Caraka instantly projected himself to his favorite chair in his room. When he opened his eyes a few seconds later, a big smile crossed his face.

According to the Eighth Lord of the Twelfth Plane, every Soul ever created has an eternal passport hidden deep down inside. This precious, celestial birthright allows access to the enormous worlds of the Almighty Creator.

And the best thing about it is that no one has to wait in a long line to apply for it.

Every being of the lower planes eventually finds
the hidden passport allowing him to
return to his Eternal Home.

31

The Ninth Lord and the Love of Others

Amazed by his inner-world journeys to the twelfth plane, the Caraka strolled over to his bed and sat down. His voyages with his recent mentors had changed the way he looked at everything, and he didn't know what to do about it. He knew he would never be the same.

He closed his eyes. Then he projected himself to the area where he normally encountered the Ten Lords. The moment he arrived he called out, "I've returned for my next class. Is the Ninth Lord ready?"

An instant later, the Caraka felt his tiny core guided in a downward direction. Down, down, down he went until he finally stopped in a zone of the twelfth plane he had never visited before.

Curious, the Caraka listened closely to the world around him. As he did, he heard what could only be described as millions upon millions of wind chimes calling out to the world around them.

Their eternal music was exhilarating. The Caraka listened intently as his new teacher announced, "Welcome young Caraka. Welcome to our magical world. You are listening to the voices of millions upon millions of giant obelisks as they convey their love to one another.

"Their precious energy is the source of the love that passes through you whenever you care for another creature of God as much as you do yourself."

Finding this incredible, the Caraka asked, "Is this the same love I feel whenever I put someone else's concerns and needs before mine?"

Happy the Caraka was on the right track, the Lord gleefully continued, "Yes! But on a much grander scale. This will be hard for you to comprehend, but the energy these enormous obelisks and I emit is the eternal love that gives one the feeling of belonging to his Almighty Creator.

"When a spiritual being fully understands this simple concept, he does everything for the good of the whole. For this reason, a tiny vibration of our love is placed in every being ever created in the worlds of God."

Wanting to learn more, the Caraka asked, "Does this mean that in order for me to feel as if I belong to our Almighty Creator, I must give to others?"

Confident that the Caraka had understood him, the Lord continued, "Yes, that's right. Our love is extremely powerful, and its eternal essence helps every being ever created to expand in ways that are impossible to do on their own.

"Love of this type guarantees that seekers of the Light and Sound go beyond the limits they place on themselves. You can see it working perfectly throughout the lower worlds."

Failing to see the big picture, the Caraka had to ask, "I recognize when humans, mammals, or reptiles give love to each other. But I fail to see it in action in other places. Can you please give me some examples of what you are talking about?"

The Ninth Lord replied, "It is simple to see this type of love everywhere you go. For example, the waters of your planet's blue oceans love the land masses that border against them immensely.

"They feel each continent's needs and do their best to work

with them wherever they can. The oceans know whenever a volcano is about to erupt and gratefully deploy their waters to guide the molten lava to where it should go. As land masses expand, this process is a demonstration of the love these giant beings have for each other.

"On a larger scale, the galaxies of the physical plane are constantly intertwining with each other to grow spiritually. To your astronomers it might appear as if they are colliding violently, but in reality they feel the same joy that two young lovers feel when they are magnetically drawn to each other.

"On an even grandeur scale, the planes of our Almighty Creator constantly share their love with each other as well. For example, the astral plane is constantly giving to the physical plane. Its powerful energy, consisting mostly of feelings and desires, helps the creators of your world nourish the suns and galaxies needed for the steady expansion going on there.

"At the same time the physical plane is constantly giving up its energy to help the astral plane replenish itself as well. Whether it be planes, suns, galaxies, oceans, or landmasses, they give to each other on a regular basis, using the same type of love you have in your heart whenever you help other creatures grow spiritually."

Astonished that these immense beings were sharing their love with each other in a way so similar to humans, the Caraka began to mull over this information.

Finding it impossible to comprehend one thing, he asked, "Where do these obelisks get their energy to share with others? Do they create it themselves? Or does it flow down to them from somewhere above the twelfth plane?"

Having already anticipated this question, the Ninth Lord continued, "The giant obelisks of my world can be considered eternal Co-Creators of the love of God. Approximately every fifty million Earth years, we Lords decide the amount of love to be created and inform the obelisks how much we need.

"If the planes below us are in a cycle of expansion we ask for more. It they're retracting, we create very little and store the incoming love on the seventh plane. Very seldom do the worlds above the seventh plane need a recalibration of energy. They are perfectly balanced and no foreseeable changes are envisioned."

Once again aware that he was in way over his head, the Caraka thought it best not to ask any more questions. Instead, he placed his attention on the celestial music surrounding him. A few Earth minutes later, the wind chime melody began to slowly fade away.

When it was impossible to hear their soft tinkling, he slowly opened his eyes and nodded his head in acknowledgement. For the first time, he understood that the loving of others as much as we love ourselves was deeply imgrained in all of us.

It had been implanted in our tiny cores, or Souls, eons ago because the Ten Lords of the Twelfth Plane had willed it to be so.

Loving others, as much as we love ourselves, is part of every spiritual being's birthright.

32

The Tenth Lord and the Love of Being an Eternal Co-worker

Certain that the Tenth Lord was waiting for him, the Caraka sat down in his chair and closed his eyes, projecting himself to the twelfth plane. So pleased that he had been able to understand just about everything these amazing beings were teaching him so far, he scanned the clear world around him. Then once again he concentrated on his inner hearing.

At first there was nothing to hear, but as he listened closer he finally heard what sounded like the loud cries of millions upon millions of eagles calling out to each other. Their screeches penetrated his inner core, and before he could figure out who or what was creating these sounds, he felt himself once again being whisked away.

On and on he traveled, until he recognized that he was being propelled toward a giant egg—a giant egg of clear energy that appeared many times larger than the physical universe. He instinctively sensed it was a site of great importance.

He finally came to a stop close to the center of the egg. Wondering what awaited him there, he placed his complete attention on the celestial music permeating the site's clear energy.

Earth seconds later, he discovered that the eagle cries were being sung on a number of different levels—all of them blending in perfectly together. Eager to learn what type of beings communicated in this manner, the Caraka continued to adjust his inner ear so he could identify them.

Moments later, he perceived trillions upon trillions of long, rectangular boxes. Each of these clear boxes floated independently and appeared to be bigger than the Milky Way galaxy.

Finding all of this incredible, the Caraka continued observing them until he discerned that they were revolving around a central point. Wanting to find out more about the site, he cautiously headed toward it.

Half way there, a loud telepathic voice called out, "Welcome little Caraka. I am the Tenth Lord. I suggest that you stop right where you are. This region is where the desires of the Ten Lords are dispersed. If you come any closer you will be automatically absorbed into one of our new creations."

Guessing that Souls could be disseminated from here to create other worlds, the Caraka asked, "Why are tiny orbs, such as me, reassigned over and over again to far off worlds? It seems as if we are sent everywhere. Will there ever be an end to our travels?"

Not at all surprised by the Caraka's question, the Tenth Lord replied, "Little one. Your inner core is the equivalent of a molecule with the capacity to be transferred just about anywhere.

"You could be compared to a drop of water falling out of the sky on your blue planet—a drop that could easily become part of one of your oceans or ever-flowing rivers. Water is one of the most important elements in the universes below us and wherever it exists, life follows.

"Tiny orbs of the Light and Sound, such as you, are just as important. Beings with your precious energy are routinely routed to all the worlds of God in order to share the love they carry.

"Not one plane below this site lacks the nourishment that exudes from your internal essence. And just like a drop of water, all of you have the potential of being amazing co-workers with God.

"This egg happens to be where your primordial energy was originally implanted with the love that allows you to become an amazing Co-worker with God. The eagle cries you hear are actually the energy which makes this all possible."

This was all way beyond him. The Caraka remained silent. He had always known that water was crucial throughout the physical plane, but had no idea that human Souls were just as important.

Wanting to learn more, the Caraka said, "Ever since I was a child, I've marveled at the miracle that occurs whenever water is added to a planted seed. But I have little understanding of what a human Soul can do. Can you tell me what little creatures like me are capable of doing?"

Almost instantly, the Caraka felt the energy around him begin to change. Then he was being propelled in a downward direction. Milliseconds later, he found himself at the border of the third and fourth planes, floating over a massive, pale yellow sea.

As he observed the effervescent body below him, a large portion of it broke away. It appeared to be headed for a world below the one he was observing. He watched in amazement as this independent body fragmented into millions of tiny yellow Souls. Souls just like him.

Captivated by the sudden appearance of these countless sparks of God, the Caraka listened closely as the telepathic voice of the Tenth Lord added, "The Souls you see have just been assigned to the upper physical plane to participate in a civilization that is rapidly expanding.

"Once they arrive there, they will be asked to receive and distribute large quantities of the Light and Sound of God—Light and Sound that is needed for the slow expansion of the upper physical plane.

"Humans are more like drops of water than you know. Wherever you little beings are assigned, you bring with you a higher level of consciousness. Your precious love forces the area to raise its vibrations. Truly, you are amazing beings.

Finding this incredulous, the Caraka queried, "On Earth, we are constantly fighting among ourselves. As we do, we inevitably destroy whatever we've created, along with other forms of life as well. How can destroying other creatures of God be good?"

Pleased with the Caraka's question, the Tenth Lord replied, "We beings of the higher worlds are constantly destroying our creations as well, and we have no problem doing so. Why? Because we are able to see the big picture.

"Unconsciously, Earthlings do the same thing. You constantly flood your planet with the Light and Sound of God. Once you've added a sufficient amount, a spiritual transformation occurs."

Finding it hard to believe that the billions of Souls living on his blue world were actually doing something positive, the Caraka timidly asked, "Why is it that most humans feel as if we are destroying ourselves and our planet, when in reality we are all doing what is required of us?"

Wanting to help the Caraka better understand humanity's spiritual assignment, the Tenth Lord replied, "Most Earthlings have no idea of the roles they play in the hierarchy of our grand Creator. They are completely unaware that they are precious conduits for the energy of God called Love.

"If they did, they would make a greater effort to consciously connect with the Light and Sound on a regular basis. This would enable them to spot the Hand of God as it guides their every move. With this type of consciousness, they would easily recognize the importance of what they are doing.

"In the near future, Earthlings will be forced to change yet again. When this occurs, the consciousness of your planet will rise, and the majority of humans will gratefully accept the important roles they play.

"Unfortunately your short class with me has come to an end. Go home little one. Return to your blue world to participate in the magical event that is about to take place there."

Appreciating all the Tenth Lord had just shared with him, the Caraka placed his attention on his favorite chair. Then he projected himself to his home. The instant he arrived he opened his eyes and looked out the window.

It was raining, and as he watched the tiny raindrops splattering against the windowpane, he thought about the precious water that nourished his home. It was hard to believe, that human Souls could be compared to raindrops—giant, multi-colored raindrops routinely assigned throughout the worlds of God—guaranteeing that spiritual civilizations receive the love they greatly need.

Tiny orbs of energy, or Souls, routinely travel throughout the worlds of God to nourish them with their special love.

33

The Next Teacher

Saddened to be finishing his classes with the Lords of the Twelfth Plane, the Caraka plopped down in his favorite chair. It was hard to believe, but these ten beings were the Creators of the Worlds of God. The way in which they shared their love and responsibilities had surprised him greatly.

Appreciating everything he had recently learned, he projected himself one final time to their site. The instant he arrived, he called out, "This is my last class, and I want to thank all of you. I had no idea that there were ten distinctive sounds of love. And that each sound is vital for the survival of God's creations."

Certain that the Caraka's Earth-bound level of consciousness was no longer the same, the First Lord replied, "We are pleased we were able to share with you a little information about the energies we wield. However, there are other worlds awaiting you. Please place your attention on your inner hearing. Then follow our celestial music to your next teacher."

Knowing this was important, the Caraka listened closely to the sounds around him. Earth seconds later, he clearly heard an enormous chorus. Its melody appeared to be coming from an area below the site where the Lords always met.

Listening more closely, he realized that this powerful sound reminded him of enormous waves crashing upon a rocky beach. It was flowing outward, similar to radio waves, getting progressively louder as it traveled farther and farther away.

These waves were passing through him in what he estimated to be five-second intervals. The Caraka quickly recognized that these waves were powerful enough to destroy him. Suddenly a giant wave, much larger than the others, lifted him up and carried him away.

Like a celestial surfer, the Caraka watched in awe as he quickly descended the planes of his Almighty Creator on this wave. When he came upon what he could only describe as a giant sun at the higher end of the Atma Lok, or Soul plane, the wave released him.

From what he could see, the enormous orb consisted of a soft, golden energy and was similar in size to three hundred galaxies of the physical plane. Wondering why the Lords of the Twelfth Plane had guided him here, the Caraka cautiously approached this giant being.

Halfway there, its soft telepathic voice called out to him, "Welcome young student from the physical plane. Welcome to the upper Soul plane. I will be your guide for your next eleven inner-world journeys. I look forward to helping you as you learn more about the amazing sites of our Grand Creator."

"As you can see, the Soul plane is enormous. It is in constant flux, serving as the buffer between the upper and lower worlds. Most of what exists here is assigned temporarily, preparing itself to be transferred to the worlds below us."

Surprised to find that he had nothing to ask this giant being, the Caraka smiled gratefully in its direction. Then he remembered an earlier inner journey where someone had told him there were three of these giant orbs in the worlds of God.

Wanting to confirm if this was true or not, the Caraka asked, "During a previous class, I was told that there are only three of you giant orbs in the worlds of God. If I remember correctly, your energy attracts smaller forms of life in order to replenish their energy, or love. Is this true?"

Pleased with the Caraka's memory, the giant orb joyfully replied, "Yes, I am capable of replenishing love. But as you shall see, I am also capable of doing much more."

Certain he was going to enjoy his new assignment, the Caraka smiled at the giant being before him. Then he just had to ask, "I also remember that you are programmed to emit the exact amount of love I need, without knocking me out of balance. If this is so, can you give me a little of your precious energy?"

Delighted to share its love with an Earthling, the golden orb joyfully replied, "You're right, little one. My energy can revitalize the love you carry in your heart. This always helps little beings like you complete your spiritual assignments.

"When initiates of the Light and Sound arrive here, many of them are being stretched to their limits. Once they merge with my energy, I could be compared to a giant battery charger, ready and willing to help them get through their extensive training and purification.

"From what I can see, your recent spiritual experiences have altered you greatly. This change of consciousness has caused you problems. Whenever a spiritual traveler from the lower worlds is allowed to pull the cosmic veil aside to partake of the love of the higher planes, he must readjust his life accordingly.

"You are no longer just a citizen of your small blue planet, but an advanced traveler with inner-world responsibilities and associations to take into account and respect. The members of the spiritual hierarchy who are guiding you now deem you part of their team and you will be called upon if needed.

"From the light you are emitting, I know you feel there is very little chance of this happening. But you are wrong! The Masters of the Light and Sound are aware of your training. They know you have the capacity to guide beings into the higher worlds, and they will eventually ask you to teach others about their eternal home and the love that awaits them there.

"They will also call upon you to share your love with the world around you, regardless whether anyone is ever aware of it. You, too, are the equivalent of a highly charged battery filled with love. And your energy is able to help others fulfill their spiritual destinies, regardless of where they currently reside in the spiritual hierarchy. Now, little one, please relax as I send you the exact amount of love you need at this moment."

Overwhelmed by the golden orb's message, the Caraka prepared himself for the energy he was about to receive. An instant later, he watched as a small shaft of golden light headed his way. The moment it struck his tiny heart, he felt its soft energy penetrate the deepest recesses of his inner core. Then it began to caress him until he felt his energy slowly balance itself out.

Suddenly feeling much better, the Caraka listened closely as the giant orb added, "This is enough for now. We will begin our classes when you return. I foresee both of us enjoying the journeys we are about to share together."

Aware that his last class had come to an end, the Caraka placed his attention on his small room on planet Earth. Opening his eyes a few seconds later, he was astonished to see a brilliant, golden light filling his room. Somehow the soft love of the giant orb had followed him home.

As he marveled at its beautiful energy, he realized that he had returned so relaxed that it was impossible for him to do anything but sit in his favorite chair and enjoy the giant orb's special recharging energy.

Every Spiritual Traveler eventually receives unexpected assignments from the Masters who trained them.

34

Training with the Lords of the Henge

Fully aware he had just completed thirty-three amazing inner-world journeys, the Caraka sat down in his favorite chair. Once he was comfortable, he gazed into his third eye and instantly spotted the image of his Master, the Ancient One.

His beloved teacher was calmly sitting alongside a small river, waiting for him. With so much to report, the Caraka joyfully called out as he headed his way, "I'm so happy to see you. I've learned so much since we last met."

Delighted that his student had finished his latest assignment, the Ancient One smiled and patted the ground at his side.

Once the Caraka was comfortably seated, the Master announced, "Your recent mentors are pleased with your efforts. Because you have done so well, you will be able to continue your advanced training.

"As you've recognized, your level of consciousness has been greatly altered. With this change comes additional responsibility. Before we discuss what this means, I need to ask you which experience impacted you the most?"

Finding this an impossible question to answer, the Caraka remained silent. Then he quickly mulled over his recent inner-world journeys with the Master of the Middle Universe, The Master of the Alaya Lok and the Ten Lords of the Twelfth Plane.

His visits to their worlds had been so incredible that it was impossible for him to pick one that stood out more than the others. Finally, his first experience with the Ten Lords of the Twelfth Plane jumped out.

Pleased he had an answer, the Caraka calmly replied, "Well, all of my experiences were amazing. But the inner-world journey that surprised me the most was the one where I first met the Ten Lords of the Twelfth Plane. I had no idea that these beings existed, nor that I would be expected to study with them."

Understanding the Caraka's surprise, the Ancient One said, "I too was taken aback when my Master led me to their amazing site five hundred thousand years ago. I had no idea they were known as the Lords of the Henge.

"Nor had I known that the different forms of love they create are what keep our Almighty Creator's worlds alive and moving in the same direction. Now that you know a little bit about them, what do you think of their responsibilities?"

Finding this question harder than the first one, the Caraka stared blankly into the distance. His limited level of consciousness always seemed to keep him from seeing the big picture. He needed help.

Quickly placing his attention on the magical site where he always found the Ten Lords, he instantly projected himself there and called out, "Hello, I've returned to ask all of you a question. My Master, the Ancient One, wants to know what I think about the responsibilities you have accepted upon yourselves. I have no idea how to answer him."

Finding it humorous that the Caraka had returned so quickly, the First Lord replied, "We Lords are no different from any other being in the worlds of God. We create what we want and accept responsibility for our creations as we go along.

"These creations, and the responsibilities that come with them, run parallel with our love—perpetually changing the amazing worlds we live in."

"Little Caraka, you too, are constantly creating your own world. This means you are responsible for everything you generate as well."

Finding the First Lord's answer quite surprising, the Caraka remained silent. He found it hard to believe that the Ten Lords were just like him, having to accept responsibility for whatever they created.

Wondering if he had gotten all of this right, the Caraka meekly smiled at the First Lord. Then he projected himself back to his body seating alongside his beloved Master.

The instant he arrived, he gazed into his teacher's eyes and said, "Well, according to the First Lord, the Ten Lords of the Henge are constantly creating and accepting their responsibilities as they go along."

Pleased with the Caraka's answer, the Ancient One nodded wisely as he added, "Yes, those amazing beings are learning just as you are. Even though they are perfect, they're accountable for the life-forms their love creates.

"Our experiences are part of their ever growing worlds and are instantly absorbed into the energy we share with them. And just like any nurturing mother on planet Earth, they watch with great anticipation as their offspring slowly learn how to fill themselves with love in order to return to their eternal home."

Feeling as if he was still missing a number of integral pieces of this extraordinary puzzle, the Caraka absent-mindedly said to himself, "The Ten Lords of the Henge are perfect, but the little beings they've created are not.

"Nevertheless, they accept responsibility for whatever happens. And with both perfect and imperfect beings, the worlds of God march on—to wherever they are going."

It was still all way beyond him. The Caraka smiled incredulously at his beloved Master. After all was said and done, everything around him appeared to be working fine. And that was all that really mattered to the humans of planet Earth and the Lords of the Henge.

Eventually, every true seeker of the Light and Sound receives higher world training with the Lords of the Henge.

Made in the USA
Coppell, TX
05 August 2022

80988824R00115